Step-by-Step
Fractions

Intermediate

Published by Instructional Fair • TS Denison
an imprint of

 **Children's Publishing**

Author: Margaret Thomas
Editors: Jerry Aten, Melissa Warner Hale

 Children's Publishing

Published by Instructional Fair • TS Denison
An imprint of McGraw-Hill Children's Publishing
Copyright © 2004 McGraw-Hill Children's Publishing

Send all inquiries to:
McGraw-Hill Children's Publishing
3195 Wilson Drive NW
Grand Rapids, Michigan 49544

Step-by-Step Fractions—intermediate
ISN: 0-7682-2636-8

1 2 3 4 5 6 7 8 9 PHXBK 09 08 07 06 05 04

Table of Contents

© McGraw-Hill Children's Publishing

0-7682-2636-8 *Step-by-Step Fractio*

Introduction

The *Step-by-Step Series* was created to help students develop a basic understanding of various math skills through practice exercises. Activities progress in difficulty based on a practical, systematic approach. Students struggle with fraction concepts. Assignments in *Fractions* focus on fractions, decimals, and percents and include fractional parts, operations involving fractions, mixed numbers and decimals, and the relationships that exist among fractions, decimals, and percents. Important fraction concepts are presented in easy-to-understand grade-appropriate exercises.

Applications include calculating perimeters, areas, weights, and tips. Math Hints, Math Facts, and Examples are included to make the exercises student-friendly. Some pages are self-checking with matching and multiple-choice answers that complete a magic square, a maze, or a riddle. A convenient eight-page pullout answer key is provided in the middle of the book.

© McGraw-Hill Children's Publishing

0-7682-2636-8 *Step-by-Step Fractions*

Fractional Shapes

Example: $\frac{3}{5}$ For every set of 5 objects, shade 3.

Shade the objects to show the fraction.

1. $\frac{1}{3}$ ☆☆☆

2. $\frac{2}{5}$ ◇◇◇◇◇

3. $\frac{4}{9}$ ☐☐☐☐☐☐☐☐☐

4. $\frac{3}{4}$ ▭▭▭▭▭▭▭▭▭▭▭▭

5. $\frac{5}{6}$ ◇◇◇◇◇◇◇◇◇◇◇◇

6. $\frac{1}{2}$ ♡♡♡♡♡♡♡♡♡♡

7. $\frac{2}{3}$ ☆☆☆☆☆☆☆☆☆

8. $\frac{1}{4}$ ◇◇◇◇◇◇◇◇◇◇◇◇

9. $\frac{4}{5}$ ☐☐☐☐☐☐☐☐☐☐

10. $\frac{1}{6}$ ▭▭▭▭▭▭▭▭▭▭▭▭▭▭▭▭▭▭

 0-7682-2636-8 *Step-by-Step Fractions*

Name_____ Date _____

Fractional Flowers

Color the petals to show the fraction.

1.

2.

3.

4.

5.

6.

7.

8.

0-7682-2636-8 Step-by-Step Fractions

Name_____ Date _____

Fraction Strips

Math Hint: The top number (numerator) gives the parts used. The bottom number (denominator) gives the number of parts in the whole.

Example: $\frac{2}{3}$ Shade 2 of the 3 parts.

Shade each strip to show the fraction.

1. $\frac{4}{5}$

2. $\frac{3}{4}$

3. $\frac{5}{6}$

4. $\frac{6}{8}$

Divide each strip into parts and shade to show the fraction.

5. $\frac{1}{4}$

6. $\frac{2}{6}$

7. $\frac{2}{5}$

8. $\frac{3}{3}$

Bonus: The shaded areas are the same for the fractions _____ and _____.

McGraw-Hill Children's Publishing   0-7682-2636-8 *Step-by-Step Fractions*

Name_____ Date _____

Garden Plot

Gilbert the Gardener is planning a garden plot for the Garfields.
Gloria Garfield wants to plant

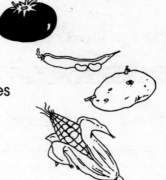

$\frac{1}{6}$ red tomatoes

$\frac{1}{4}$ green beans

$\frac{1}{3}$ orange sweet potatoes

$\frac{1}{8}$ purple eggplants

$\frac{1}{12}$ yellow corn

Gilbert decided that each type of vegetable should be
grouped together. He also thinks there might be room for a
brown bench.

Help Gilbert design a garden for the Garfields by shading the
appropriate amount of vegetable colors in the grid below.

Is there space for a garden bench? _____ If so, what fraction o

the garden is available for the bench? _____

                    0-7682-2636-8 *Step-by-Step Fraction*

Capital Fractions

Find the capital city by solving the fraction problems. Use the city clues to name the state.

1. Capital: _____

   first $\frac{1}{4}$ of San Diego

   first $\frac{1}{10}$ of Chula Vista

   third $\frac{1}{4}$ of La Mirada

   first $\frac{3}{7}$ of Mendota

   last $\frac{2}{7}$ of Modesto

State: _____

2. Capital: _____

   second $\frac{1}{4}$ of Alma

   first $\frac{1}{4}$ of Ann Arbor

   last $\frac{1}{5}$ of Niles

   middle $\frac{1}{3}$ of Ludington

State: _____

3. Capital: _____

   fifth $\frac{1}{6}$ of Niagara Falls

   third $\frac{1}{6}$ of Albion

   last $\frac{2}{5}$ of Olean

   last $\frac{1}{4}$ of Troy

State: _____

Fill in the missing fractions.

4. Capital: Austin

   second _____ of Dallas

   second _____ of Lubbock

   third _____ of Fort Stockton

   second _____ of Edinburg

State: _____

0-7682-2636-8 Step-by-Step Fractions

Fraction Tower

Complete the strips by labeling each fraction mark.

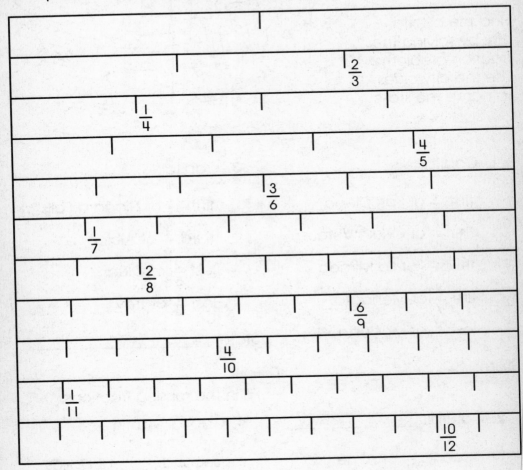

Math Fact: Numbers such as $\frac{1}{4}$, $\frac{2}{8}$, and $\frac{3}{12}$ that are directly above each other are called equivalent fractions.

The fractions equivalent to $\frac{1}{2}$ are _____.

The fractions equivalent to $\frac{2}{3}$ are _____.

10

0-7682-2636-8 *Step-by-Step Fractions*

Walking the Line

Place the letter associated with each fraction above its location on the number line.

Example: N $\frac{2}{9}$

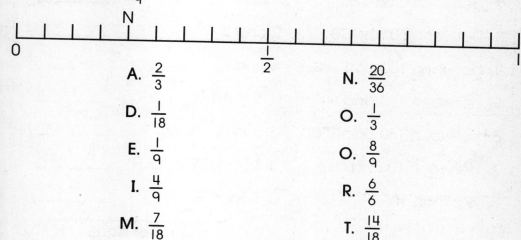

A. $\frac{2}{3}$		**N.** $\frac{20}{36}$	
D. $\frac{1}{18}$		**O.** $\frac{1}{3}$	
E. $\frac{1}{9}$		**O.** $\frac{8}{9}$	
I. $\frac{4}{9}$		**R.** $\frac{6}{6}$	
M. $\frac{7}{18}$		**T.** $\frac{14}{18}$	

Math Hint: Think of 1 as $\frac{18}{18}$.

Check It! The letters above the number line complete the

statement: The _____ gives the number of

equal parts in a whole object.

Name_____ Date _____

Who's Who

Cross out each answer in the Answer Bank. Two of the remaining numbers are factors of the third.

Divisible by	Rule
2	Number ends in 0, 2, 4, 6, 8
3	Sum of the digits is divisible by 3
4	Number formed by last two digits is divisible by 4
5	Number ends in 0 or 5
9	Sum of the digits is divisible by 9
10	Number ends in 0

I'm	**Divisible By**	**Who Am I?**
1. between 80 and 90	9	_____
2. between 0 and 50	5 and 9	_____
3. between 60 and 70	2 and 3	_____
4. between 100 and 150	5 and 9	_____
5. between 750 and 800	3, 4, and 10	_____
6. between 160 and 180	3 and 4, but not 9	_____
7. between 10 and 30	3, but not 2, 5, or 9	_____
8. less than 100	2, 5, and 9	_____

Answer Bank

66   780   168   22

45   770   81

21   35   135   90

Bonus: _____ x _____ = _____

0-7682-2636-8 *Step-by-Step Fractions*

GCF Diagrams

Example: GCF of 36 and 54 is 18.

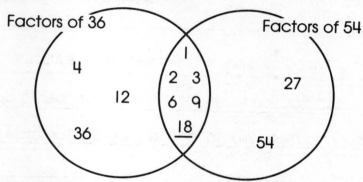

Math Hint: 3 and 6 are factors of 18 because 3 x 6 = 18. There are four other factors of 18.

Complete the diagrams. Be sure to include all factors of the numbers. Underline the GCF.

1. 18 and 24

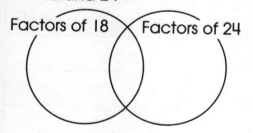

3. 21 and 42

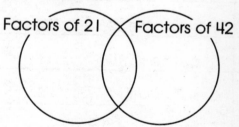

2. 30 and 45

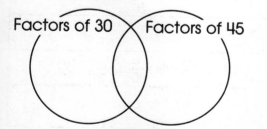

4. 10 and 27

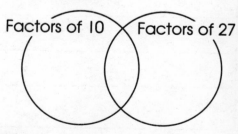

© McGraw-Hill Children's Publishing

0-7682-2636-8 *Step-by-Step Fractions*

As Simple As...

Mattie Matics was confused when she took this quiz. Find and correct her 6 errors.

QUIZ: Simplifying Fractions   **Name:** Mattie Matics

Reduce each fraction to lowest terms. Remember to divide numerator and denominator by the greatest common factor.

1. $\dfrac{2}{10} = \dfrac{1}{8}$ 7. $\dfrac{25}{60} = \dfrac{5}{10}$

2. $\dfrac{4}{6} = \dfrac{2}{3}$ 8. $\dfrac{8}{20} = \dfrac{4}{5}$

3. $\dfrac{6}{8} = \dfrac{3}{4}$ 9. $\dfrac{12}{42} = \dfrac{2}{7}$

4. $\dfrac{4}{10} = \dfrac{1}{6}$ 10. $\dfrac{22}{77} = \dfrac{2}{7}$

5. $\dfrac{18}{27} = \dfrac{1}{9}$ 11. $\dfrac{30}{45} = \dfrac{10}{15}$

6. $\dfrac{15}{25} = \dfrac{3}{5}$ 12. $\dfrac{5}{100} = \dfrac{1}{20}$

14

One Bad Apple

Reduce each fraction to lowest terms. Connect each apple to its basket. Circle the "one bad apple."

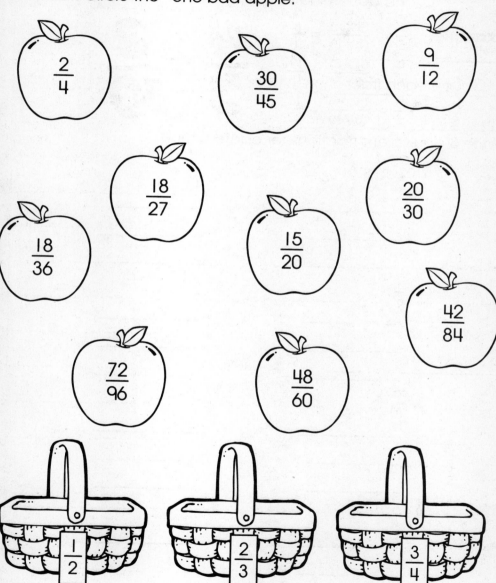

0-7682-2636-8 *Step-by-Step Fractions*

Equivalent Fractions

Math Hint: To write equivalent fractions, multiply the numerator and denominator by the same number.

Example: $\frac{4}{5} = \frac{(4 \times 2)}{(5 \times 2)} = \frac{8}{10}$

$\frac{4}{5} = \frac{(4 \times 3)}{(5 \times 3)} = \frac{12}{15}$

$\frac{4}{5} = \frac{(4 \times 4)}{(5 \times 4)} = \frac{16}{20}$

Write 3 equivalent fractions for each number.

1. $\frac{2}{3}$

_____

_____

_____

2. $\frac{3}{5}$

_____

_____

_____

3. $\frac{9}{10}$

_____

_____

_____

4. $\frac{4}{9}$

_____

_____

_____

5. $\frac{1}{4}$

_____

_____

_____

6. $\frac{2}{5}$

_____

_____

_____

7. $\frac{1}{2}$

_____

_____

_____

8. $\frac{3}{10}$

_____

_____

_____

0-7682-2636-8 *Step-by-Step Fraction*

All Mixed Up!

Improper fraction = a fraction with numerator ≥ denominator. To write an improper fraction as a mixed number, divide the denominator into the numerator.

Example: $\frac{13}{5}$
$$5\overline{)13} \quad 2\frac{3}{5}$$
$$-10$$
$$3$$

Half of the mixed numbers are "mixed up." Correct them.

1. $\frac{4}{3} = 1\frac{1}{4}$

6. $\frac{27}{4} = 7\frac{3}{4}$

2. $\frac{7}{2} = 3\frac{1}{2}$

7. $\frac{8}{3} = 2\frac{1}{8}$

3. $\frac{100}{11} = 9\frac{1}{11}$

8. $\frac{60}{9} = 6\frac{2}{3}$

4. $\frac{5}{2} = 2\frac{1}{5}$

9. $\frac{75}{24} = 3\frac{3}{8}$

5. $\frac{12}{5} = 2\frac{2}{5}$

10. $\frac{35}{3} = 11\frac{2}{3}$

0-7682-2636-8 *Step-by-Step Fractions*

Fraction Buzz

Math Hint: Multiply the denominator by the whole number and add the numerator.

Example: $2\frac{3}{4} = \frac{(4 \times 2 + 3)}{4} = \frac{11}{4}$

Connect each bee to its flower.

0-7682-2636-8 *Step-by-Step Fractions*

Fraction Bench Marks

Connect the pigeon's number with the seat containing the closest number.

Math Hints:

Numerator almost equal to denominator → almost 1.

Numerator small compared to denominator → almost 0.

Numerator about half of denominator → almost $\frac{1}{2}$.

19

Name_____ Date _____

Like Denominators
Like Measurements

Math Hint: To add fractions with the same (like) denominator, add the numerators and use the common denominator. Reduce to lowest terms if possible.

Example: $\frac{5}{12} + \frac{1}{12} = \frac{6}{12}$ or $\frac{1}{2}$ $\frac{3}{7} + \frac{2}{7} = \frac{5}{7}$

Why? Denominators are similar to units of measure.
   5 inches + 1 inch = 6 inches
   5 twelfths + 1 twelfth = 6 twelfths

Complete each statement. Add the fractions.

1. $\frac{2}{5} + \frac{1}{5} =$ _____

   2 fifths + 1 _____= ___ fifths

2. $\frac{2}{9} + \frac{5}{9} =$ _____

   2 _____+ 5 _____ = ___ _____

3. $\frac{1}{15} + \frac{7}{15} =$ _____

   ___ fifteenth + ___ _____ = ___ _____

4. $\frac{3}{10} + \frac{1}{10} =$ _____

   ___ _____ + ___ _____ = ___ _____

Add.

5. $\frac{7}{11} + \frac{2}{11} =$ _____

6. $\frac{3}{20} + \frac{7}{20} =$ _____

7. $\frac{11}{25} + \frac{12}{25} =$ _____

8. $\frac{23}{50} + \frac{17}{50} =$ _____

20

Proper Fractions

Example: $\frac{3}{4} + \frac{3}{4} = \frac{6}{4} = 1\frac{2}{4}$ or $1\frac{1}{2}$

Add. Reduce to lowest terms if possible. Cross out the answers below. Complete the statement with the remaining letters.

1. $\frac{3}{5} + \frac{4}{5} =$

2. $\frac{2}{7} + \frac{5}{7} =$

3. $\frac{7}{8} + \frac{3}{8} =$

4. $\frac{16}{25} + \frac{11}{25} =$

5. $\frac{13}{20} + \frac{17}{20} =$

6. $\frac{8}{9} + \frac{8}{9} =$

7. $\frac{7}{10} + \frac{9}{10} =$

8. $\frac{23}{24} + \frac{17}{24} =$

9. $\frac{11}{15} + \frac{7}{15} =$

$1\frac{7}{9}$	$1\frac{8}{9}$	$1\frac{1}{2}$	$1\frac{1}{5}$	$1\frac{1}{25}$	$1\frac{3}{5}$
NO	AL	TT	HE	WA	ON
$1\frac{1}{4}$	$1\frac{5}{6}$	$1\frac{2}{9}$	$1\frac{2}{5}$	$1\frac{9}{10}$	$1\frac{2}{3}$
LY	YS	LE	SW	SS	ER
$1\frac{7}{10}$	$1\frac{1}{3}$	1	$1\frac{7}{25}$	$1\frac{2}{25}$	$1\frac{1}{6}$
TH	AN	E	TW	OT	O

The sum of two proper fractions is

___ ___ ___ ___ ___   ___ ___ ___ ___

___ ___ ___ ___ ___   ___ ___ ___.

21

Fraction Subtraction

Math Hint: To subtract fractions with the same (like) denominator, subtract the numerators and use the common denominator. Reduce to lowest terms.

Example: $\frac{5}{12} - \frac{1}{12} = \frac{4}{12}$ or $\frac{1}{3}$ $\qquad$ $\frac{3}{7} - \frac{2}{7} = \frac{1}{7}$

Why? Denominators are like units of measure.

5 inches – 1 inch = 4 inches
5 twelfths – 1 twelfth = 4 twelfths

Complete each statement. Subtract the fractions.

1. $\frac{2}{5} - \frac{1}{5} =$ _____

   2 fifths – 1 _____ = ___ fifth

2. $\frac{7}{9} - \frac{5}{9} =$ _____

   7 _____ – 5 _____ = __ _____

3. $\frac{7}{15} - \frac{2}{15} =$ _____

   __ _____ – __ _____ = __ _____

4. $\frac{3}{10} - \frac{1}{10} =$ _____

   __ _____ – __ _____ = __ _____

Subtract.

5. $\frac{7}{11} - \frac{2}{11} =$ _____

6. $\frac{7}{20} - \frac{3}{20} =$ _____

7. $\frac{17}{25} - \frac{11}{25} =$ _____

8. $\frac{23}{50} - \frac{17}{50} =$ _____

22

F.Y.I. Concerning LCMs

Math Hints: The *least common multiple (LCM)* of a set of numbers is the smallest number divisible by the set of numbers.

To find the LCM: 1. List the multiples of each number.
2. Find the smallest common multiple.

Example: LCM of 6 and 9   6: 6, 12, 18, 24, 30, 36, ...
9: 9, 18, 27, 36, ...
LCM is 36.

Find the LCM for each set of numbers.

1. 5 and 6

2. 4 and 7

3. 8 and 10

4. 9 and 12

5. 10 and 15

6. 12 and 20

7. 14 and 21

8. 18 and 27

9. 4, 5, and 6

10. 40, 50, and 60

Bonus: How are the answers to problems 9 and 10 related?

0-7682-2636-8 *Step-by-Step Fractions*

Name_____ Date _____

Addition: Unlike Denominators

Math Hint:
1. Find the *least common multiple* of the denominators.
2. Write equivalent fractions using the common denominator.
3. Add the fractions.
4. Simplify the answer.

Why? Denominators are like units of measure.
You must have common units of measure to add.
4 ft. + 6 in. = 48 in. + 6 in. = 54 in.

Example: $\frac{3}{4} + \frac{2}{3} =$ 1. LCM of 4 and 3 is 12.

2. $\frac{3}{4} = \frac{9}{12}$ and $\frac{2}{3} = \frac{8}{12}$

3. $\frac{9}{12} + \frac{8}{12} = \frac{17}{12}$

4. $1\frac{5}{12}$

Add.

1. $\frac{3}{5} + \frac{1}{4} =$

2. $\frac{2}{5} + \frac{9}{10} =$

3. $\frac{7}{10} + \frac{7}{15} =$

4. $\frac{5}{14} + \frac{3}{7} =$

5. $\frac{7}{8} + \frac{11}{12} =$

6. $\frac{8}{9} + \frac{5}{12} =$

7. $\frac{12}{25} + \frac{37}{50} =$

8. $\frac{3}{8} + \frac{9}{20} =$

24

0-7682-2636-8 *Step-by-Step Fractions*

Tic-Tac-Toe

Find the sum of each row, column, and diagonal. Circle the
Tic-Tac-Toe of three fractions having a sum of 1.

1.

$\frac{3}{4}$	$\frac{1}{2}$	$\frac{1}{2}$	____
$\frac{1}{4}$	$\frac{3}{8}$	$\frac{5}{8}$	____
$\frac{1}{8}$	$\frac{4}{4}$	$\frac{7}{8}$	____

____   ____   ____

2.

$\frac{1}{3}$	$\frac{1}{4}$	$\frac{11}{12}$	____
$\frac{5}{12}$	$\frac{1}{6}$	$\frac{3}{4}$	____
$\frac{1}{2}$	$\frac{7}{12}$	$\frac{5}{6}$	____

____   ____   ____

3.

$\frac{2}{5}$	$\frac{4}{15}$	$\frac{1}{10}$	____
$\frac{3}{10}$	$\frac{3}{5}$	$\frac{11}{15}$	____
$\frac{7}{15}$	$\frac{1}{3}$	$\frac{1}{5}$	____

____   ____   ____

25

© McGraw-Hill Children's Publishing

0-7682-2636-8 *Step-by-Step Fractions*

Subtraction: Unlike Denominators

Math Hint:
1. Find the *least common multiple* of the denominators.
2. Write equivalent fractions using the common denominator.
3. Subtract the fractions.
4. Simplify the answer.

Why? Denominators are like units of measure.
You must have common units of measure to subtract.
4 ft. – 6 in. = 48 in. – 6 in. = 42 in.

Example: $\frac{3}{4} - \frac{2}{3} =$ 1. LCM of 3 and 4 is 12.

2. $\frac{3}{4} = \frac{9}{12}$ and $\frac{2}{3} = \frac{8}{12}$

3. $\frac{9}{12} - \frac{8}{12} = \frac{1}{12}$

Subtract.

1. $\frac{3}{5} - \frac{1}{6} =$

2. $\frac{2}{9} - \frac{1}{10} =$

3. $\frac{7}{15} - \frac{2}{5} =$

4. $\frac{5}{14} - \frac{2}{7} =$

5. $\frac{7}{8} - \frac{2}{5} =$

6. $\frac{8}{9} - \frac{5}{6} =$

7. $\frac{12}{25} - \frac{17}{50} =$

8. $\frac{3}{8} - \frac{3}{20} =$

26

Name_____ Date _____

Magic Square Fractions

The sum of each row, column, and diagonal of a Magic Square is the same. Use each of the following numbers once to complete the Magic Square.

$\frac{1}{8}$ $\frac{5}{24}$ $\frac{1}{4}$ $\frac{1}{3}$ $\frac{3}{8}$

$\frac{1}{6}$		
		$\frac{1}{24}$
$\frac{1}{12}$	$\frac{7}{24}$	

Hint #1: The Magic Sum is $\frac{5}{8}$.

Hint #2: Find a common denominator and rewrite the fractions.

27

        0-7682-2636-8 *Step-by-Step Fractions*

Name_____ Date _____

When There Is Too Much or Too Little

Math Hint: To simplify a mixed number containing an improper fraction, write the fraction as a mixed number and add.

$$7\frac{5}{4} = 7 + 1\frac{1}{4} = 8\frac{1}{4}$$

1. $9\frac{14}{8} = $ _____

2. $6\frac{5}{3} = $ _____

3. $12\frac{9}{5} = $ _____

4. $2\frac{19}{15} = $ _____

Math Hint: To write a whole number as a mixed number, borrow 1 and write it as a fraction.

$$8 = 7 + 1 = 7\frac{2}{2} \text{ or } 7\frac{3}{3} \text{ or } 7\frac{4}{4} \text{ , etc.}$$

5. $7 = 6\frac{}{8}$

6. $4 = 3\frac{}{9}$

7. $12 = 11\frac{}{3}$

8. $10 = $ _____ $\frac{}{2}$

Math Hint: To change a mixed number, borrow 1 and rewrite the fraction.

$$9\frac{2}{5} = 8 + 1 + \frac{2}{5} = 8 + \frac{5}{5} + \frac{2}{5} = 8\frac{7}{5}$$

9. $4\frac{1}{3} = 3$ _____

10. $9\frac{4}{5} = 8$ _____

11. $12\frac{2}{9} = $ ___ _____

12. $3\frac{1}{10} = $ ___ _____

28

0-7682-2636-8 Step-by-Step Fractions

Addition: Mixed Numbers With Like Denominators

Add the whole number parts and add the fraction parts.
Reduce to lowest terms if possible.

Example:

$$6\frac{3}{8}$$
$$+\ 7\frac{1}{8}$$
$$\overline{13\frac{4}{8}} = 13\frac{1}{2}$$

1. $9\frac{2}{7}$
    $+\ 7\frac{3}{7}$
    _____

5. $20\frac{7}{15}$
    $+\ 10\frac{2}{15}$
    _____

2. $4\frac{5}{9}$
    $+\ 8\frac{1}{9}$
    _____

6. $19\frac{3}{20}$
    $+\ 1\frac{7}{20}$
    _____

3. $2\frac{1}{10}$
    $+\ 10\frac{3}{10}$
    _____

7. $8\frac{2}{9}$
    $+\ 6\frac{4}{9}$
    _____

4. $3\frac{2}{11}$
    $+\ 2\frac{3}{11}$
    _____

8. $15\frac{3}{10}$
    $+\ 14\frac{1}{10}$
    _____

0-7682-2636-8 *Step-by-Step Fractions*

Name_____ Date _____

Falling Fractions

Math Hint: If the answer contains an improper fraction, change it to a mixed number and add.

Example:

$$7 \frac{3}{4}$$
$$+ 5 \frac{3}{4}$$
$$\overline{12 \frac{6}{4}} = 12 \frac{3}{2} = 12 + 1 \frac{1}{2} = 13 \frac{1}{2}$$

1. **A** $5 \frac{3}{5}$
$+ 3 \frac{4}{5}$

4. **O** $6 \frac{21}{25}$
$+ 2 \frac{19}{25}$

7. **V** $4 \frac{7}{11}$
$+ 4 \frac{9}{11}$

2. **E** $2 \frac{7}{9}$
$+ 3 \frac{5}{9}$

5. **P** $7 \frac{3}{4}$
$+ 1 \frac{3}{4}$

8. **Y** $6 \frac{7}{15}$
$+ 1 \frac{11}{15}$

3. **H** $1 \frac{7}{8}$
$+ 2 \frac{5}{8}$

6. **T** $2 \frac{2}{7}$
$+ 5 \frac{5}{7}$

Why did $\frac{12}{7}$ keep falling over? It was

$\overline{}$ $\overline{}$ $\overline{}$ $\overline{}$ $\overline{}$ $\overline{}$ $\overline{}$ $\overline{}$
8 $9\frac{3}{5}$ $9\frac{1}{2}$ $4\frac{1}{2}$ $6\frac{1}{3}$ $9\frac{2}{5}$ $9\frac{5}{11}$ $8\frac{1}{5}$

0-7682-2636-8 *Step-by-Step Fractions*

Name_____ Date _____

Word to the Wise

Math Hint: Rewrite the mixed numbers using a common denominator.

Example:

$$6\tfrac{1}{3} \qquad 6\tfrac{2}{6}$$
$$+7\tfrac{1}{6} \qquad +7\tfrac{1}{6}$$
$$\overline{} \qquad \overline{13\tfrac{3}{6} = 13\tfrac{1}{2}}$$

Add. Cross out the answers below. Use the remaining letters to complete the statement at the bottom of the page.

1.
$$2\tfrac{2}{5}$$
$$+7\tfrac{1}{4}$$

3.
$$2\tfrac{1}{8}$$
$$+10\tfrac{3}{5}$$

5.
$$20\tfrac{4}{15}$$
$$+10\tfrac{2}{5}$$

2.
$$6\tfrac{1}{6}$$
$$+8\tfrac{2}{3}$$

4.
$$7\tfrac{2}{3}$$
$$+8\tfrac{1}{9}$$

6.
$$12\tfrac{1}{2}$$
$$+13\tfrac{1}{6}$$

$14\tfrac{5}{6}$	$14\tfrac{3}{3}$	$25\tfrac{2}{3}$	$25\tfrac{5}{6}$	$12\tfrac{6}{7}$	$12\tfrac{29}{40}$
EPL	EDU	ACE	CET	OLO	THE
$30\tfrac{5}{6}$	$15\tfrac{2}{3}$	$30\tfrac{2}{3}$	$9\tfrac{4}{5}$	$15\tfrac{7}{9}$	$9\tfrac{13}{20}$
WES	TTE	TOP	RMS	NUM	BER

Remember: R __ __ __ __ __ __   __ __

__ __ __ __ __ __ __   __ __ __ __ __ __ __ __.

31

0-7682-2636-8 Step-by-Step Fractions

Seven-Eleven

Rewrite the mixed numbers using a common denominator. If the answer contains an improper fraction, change it to a mixed number and add.

Example:

$$5 \frac{5}{7} \qquad 5 \frac{30}{42}$$

$$+ 5 \frac{5}{6} \qquad + 5 \frac{35}{42}$$

$$10 \frac{65}{42} = 10 + 1 \frac{23}{42} = 11 \frac{23}{42}$$

1. $9 \frac{3}{5}$
    $+ 1 \frac{4}{7}$

4. $6 \frac{21}{25}$
    $+ 1 \frac{19}{50}$

7. $3 \frac{3}{4}$
    $+ 7 \frac{15}{16}$

2. $10 \frac{7}{9}$
    $+ 3 \frac{5}{6}$

5. $11 \frac{18}{35}$
    $+ 12 \frac{4}{5}$

3. $8 \frac{7}{8}$
    $+ 2 \frac{3}{4}$

6. $6 \frac{2}{3}$
    $+ 4 \frac{4}{5}$

Check It! What do the seven answers have in common?

_____

32

0-7682-2636-8 Step-by-Step Fractions

Name_____ Date _____

Diet Dilemma

Math Hint: Subtract the whole numbers and subtract the fraction parts.

Example:

$$9\frac{3}{8}$$
$$-7\frac{1}{8}$$
$$2\frac{2}{8} = 2\frac{1}{4}$$

Subtract. Reduce to lowest terms if possible. Cross out the correct answers and complete the sentence with the remaining letters.

1. $9\frac{5}{7}$
   $-7\frac{1}{7}$

3. $12\frac{7}{10}$
   $-10\frac{3}{10}$

5. $20\frac{7}{15}$
   $-10\frac{2}{15}$

7. $20\frac{6}{7}$
   $-15\frac{2}{7}$

2. $10\frac{5}{9}$
   $-8\frac{1}{9}$

4. $3\frac{8}{11}$
   $-2\frac{3}{11}$

6. $19\frac{11}{20}$
   $-12\frac{7}{20}$

8. $9\frac{2}{3}$
   $-4\frac{1}{3}$

$2\frac{2}{5}$ TO	$10\frac{5}{6}$ AL	$10\frac{1}{3}$ OS	$5\frac{2}{7}$ RE	$5\frac{1}{4}$ AD
$2\frac{4}{7}$ MA	$2\frac{4}{9}$ LL	$5\frac{3}{7}$ YR	$7\frac{1}{5}$ TO	$1\frac{1}{5}$ ED
$2\frac{1}{5}$ UC	$1\frac{5}{11}$ BE	$5\frac{4}{7}$ GI	$7\frac{1}{4}$ ED	$5\frac{1}{3}$ NS

Why did $2\frac{1}{4}$ have trouble losing more weight?

It was __ __ __ __ __ __ __ __ __ __ __ __ __ __ __ __ __.

33

© McGraw-Hill Children's Publishing

0-7682-2636-8 *Step-by-Step Fractions*

Seeing Double

Math Hint: Borrow 1 from the whole number.

Example: $7\frac{1}{4}$ $6\frac{5}{4}$ **Note:** $7\frac{1}{4} = 6 + 1\frac{1}{4} = 6\frac{5}{4}$

$-4\frac{3}{4}$ $-4\frac{3}{4}$

$2\frac{2}{4} = 2\frac{1}{2}$

Subtract. Reduce answers to lowest terms.

1. $9\frac{3}{5}$ 3. $12\frac{3}{8}$ 5. $16\frac{5}{11}$ 7. $20\frac{7}{15}$

$-3\frac{4}{5}$ $-8\frac{5}{8}$ $-7\frac{8}{11}$ $-8\frac{11}{15}$

2. $5\frac{4}{9}$ 4. $16\frac{2}{25}$ 6. $15\frac{7}{12}$ 8. $3\frac{1}{8}$

$-1\frac{7}{9}$ $-11\frac{23}{25}$ $-12\frac{11}{12}$ $-1\frac{7}{8}$

Check It! What do the answers have in common (hint: look at the page title)?

_____

0-7682-2636-8 *Step-by-Step Fractions*

Subtracting Mixed Numbers

Rewrite the mixed numbers using a common denominator.

Example:

$$9\frac{4}{5} \qquad 9\frac{32}{40}$$

$$-7\frac{3}{8} \qquad -7\frac{15}{40}$$

$$\overline{\qquad\qquad 2\frac{17}{40}}$$

Subtract. Cross out the answers below and complete the statement with the remaining letters.

1. $9\frac{2}{5}$
   $-7\frac{1}{4}$

3. $2\frac{3}{8}$
   $-1\frac{1}{5}$

5. $18\frac{7}{15}$
   $-10\frac{2}{5}$

7. $8\frac{5}{12}$
   $-2\frac{1}{3}$

2. $6\frac{5}{6}$
   $-1\frac{2}{3}$

4. $7\frac{2}{3}$
   $-3\frac{1}{9}$

6. $12\frac{1}{2}$
   $-3\frac{1}{3}$

$2\frac{3}{20}$	$2\frac{1}{10}$	$9\frac{1}{6}$	$9\frac{1}{3}$	$8\frac{1}{15}$	$1\frac{7}{40}$	$1\frac{2}{5}$
OWE	EAS	STM	TCO	ULT	IPL	MMO
$4\frac{1}{3}$	$8\frac{1}{5}$	$4\frac{5}{9}$	$6\frac{1}{3}$	$5\frac{1}{6}$	$6\frac{2}{3}$	$6\frac{1}{12}$
NDE	NOM	ENE	INA	EDE	TOR	ENT

Use the I __ __ __ __   __ __ __ __ __ __

__ __ __ __ __ __ __ __ __ __ __ __.

0-7682-2636-8 *Step-by-Step Fractions*

Name_____ Date _____

Improper Magic

Math Hint: If you can't subtract the fractions, borrow 1 from the whole number.

Example:

$$7\frac{1}{5} \;=\; 7\frac{4}{20} \;=\; 6\frac{24}{20}$$
$$-\,4\frac{3}{4} \;=\; -\,4\frac{15}{20} \;=\; -\,4\frac{15}{20}$$
$$=\; 2\frac{9}{20}$$

Solve the problems to complete the Magic Square and find the Magic Sum. Make sure each row, column, and diagonal has the same sum.

$14\frac{5}{24} - 5\frac{7}{8}$	$7 - 5\frac{23}{24}$	$12\frac{1}{8} - 5\frac{7}{8}$
$6\frac{1}{12} - 2\frac{23}{24}$	$10\frac{1}{8} - 4\frac{11}{12}$	$12\frac{1}{8} - 4\frac{5}{6}$
$8\frac{1}{24} - 3\frac{7}{8}$	$15\frac{5}{24} - 5\frac{5}{6}$	$3\frac{5}{6} - 1\frac{3}{4}$

The Magic Sum is _____.

36

Answer Key

Fractional Shapes 5
1. 1 star shaded
2. 2 diamonds shaded
3. 4 squares shaded
4. 6 rectangles shaded
5. 10 diamonds shaded
6. 5 hearts shaded
7. 6 stars shaded
8. 3 diamonds shaded
9. 8 squares shaded
10. 3 rectangles shaded

Fractional Flowers 6
1. 4 petals shaded
2. 3 petals shaded
3. 6 petals shaded
4. 6 petals shaded
5. 7 petals shaded
6. 3 petals shaded
7. 3 petals shaded
8. 6 petals shaded

Fraction Strips..............................7
1. $\frac{4}{5}$

2. $\frac{3}{4}$

3. $\frac{5}{6}$

4. $\frac{6}{8}$

Divide each strip into parts and shade to show the fraction.

5. $\frac{1}{4}$

6. $\frac{2}{6}$

7. $\frac{2}{5}$

8. $\frac{3}{3}$

Bonus: $\frac{3}{4}$ and $\frac{6}{8}$.

Garden Plot 8
$\frac{1}{6}$ Red tomatoes
$\frac{1}{4}$ Green beans
$\frac{1}{3}$ Orange sweet potatoes
$\frac{1}{8}$ Purple eggplants
$\frac{1}{12}$ Yellow corn

Brown bench: Yes, $\frac{1}{24}$ of garden
Possible answer

R	R	O	O	O	O
R	R	O	O	O	O
G	G	G	S	S	Y
G	G	G	S	B	Y

© McGraw-Hill Children's Publishing

Capital Fractions..............................9
1. SACRAMENTO
   California
2. LANSING
   Michigan
3. ALBANY
   New York
4. $\frac{1}{6}$
   $\frac{1}{7}$
   $\frac{1}{6}$
   $\frac{1}{4}$
   Texas

Fraction Tower..............................10

$\frac{1}{2}$ is equivalent to $\frac{2}{4}$, $\frac{3}{6}$, $\frac{4}{8}$, $\frac{5}{10}$, $\frac{6}{12}$
$\frac{2}{3}$ is equivalent to $\frac{4}{6}$, $\frac{6}{9}$, $\frac{8}{12}$

Walking the Line..............................11

D E N O M I N A T O R
0 .... $\frac{1}{2}$ 1

Who's Who..............................12
1. 81
2. 45
3. 66
4. 135
5. 780
6. 168
7. 21
8. 90
Bonus: 22 x 35 = 770

0-7682-2636-8 *Step-by-Step Fractions*

Answer Key

GCF Diagrams 13

1. Factors of 18 only: 9, 18
   Factors of 24 only: 4, 8, 12, 24
   Common factors: 1, 2, 3, 6
   GCF: 6
2. Factors of 30 only: 2, 6, 10, 30
   Factors of 45 only: 9, 45
   Common factors: 1, 3, 5, 15
   GCF: 15
3. Factors of 21 only: None
   Factors of 42 only: 2, 6, 14, 42
   Common factors: 1, 3, 7, 21
   GCF: 21
4. Factors of 10 only: 2, 5, 10
   Factors of 27 only: 3, 9, 27
   Common factors: 1
   GCF: 1

As Simple As 14
Corrected Errors

1. $\frac{1}{5}$
4. $\frac{2}{5}$
5. $\frac{2}{3}$
7. $\frac{5}{12}$
8. $\frac{2}{5}$
11. $\frac{2}{3}$

One Bad Apple 15

$\frac{1}{2}$ basket: $\frac{2}{4}$, $\frac{18}{36}$, $\frac{42}{84}$
$\frac{2}{3}$ basket: $\frac{30}{45}$, $\frac{18}{27}$, $\frac{20}{30}$
$\frac{3}{4}$ basket: $\frac{9}{12}$, $\frac{15}{20}$, $\frac{72}{96}$
One bad apple: $\frac{48}{60}$

Equivalent Fractions 16
Possible answers

1. $\frac{4}{6}$, $\frac{6}{9}$, $\frac{8}{12}$
2. $\frac{6}{10}$, $\frac{9}{15}$, $\frac{12}{20}$
3. $\frac{18}{20}$, $\frac{27}{30}$, $\frac{36}{40}$
4. $\frac{8}{18}$, $\frac{12}{27}$, $\frac{16}{36}$
5. $\frac{2}{8}$, $\frac{3}{12}$, $\frac{4}{16}$
6. $\frac{4}{10}$, $\frac{6}{15}$, $\frac{8}{20}$
7. $\frac{2}{4}$, $\frac{3}{6}$, $\frac{4}{8}$
8. $\frac{6}{20}$, $\frac{9}{30}$, $\frac{12}{40}$

All Mixed Up! 17
Corrected "Mixed Up" Answers

1. $1\frac{1}{3}$
4. $2\frac{1}{2}$
6. $6\frac{3}{4}$
7. $2\frac{2}{3}$
9. $3\frac{1}{8}$

Fraction Buzz 18
Flower → Bee

$3\frac{1}{2}$ → $\frac{7}{2}$
$4\frac{2}{3}$ → $\frac{14}{3}$
$3\frac{1}{3}$ → $\frac{10}{3}$
$2\frac{1}{6}$ → $\frac{13}{6}$
$5\frac{7}{8}$ → $\frac{47}{8}$
$6\frac{5}{8}$ → $\frac{53}{8}$
$10\frac{1}{9}$ → $\frac{91}{9}$
$8\frac{7}{9}$ → $\frac{79}{9}$

Fraction Bench Marks 19
0 bench mark: $\frac{1}{10}$, $\frac{3}{50}$, $\frac{21}{550}$
$\frac{1}{2}$ bench mark: $\frac{6}{13}$, $\frac{8}{15}$, $\frac{45}{48}$
1 bench mark: $\frac{11}{12}$, $\frac{15}{14}$, $\frac{98}{100}$

Like Denominators → Like Measurements .. 20

1. $\frac{3}{5}$; fifths; 3
2. $\frac{7}{9}$; ninths; ninths; 7 ninths
3. $\frac{8}{15}$; 1; 7 fifteenths; 8 fifteenths
4. $\frac{4}{10}$ or $\frac{2}{5}$; 3 tenths; 1 tenth; 4 tenths
5. $\frac{10}{11}$
6. $\frac{10}{20}$ or $\frac{1}{2}$
7. $\frac{23}{25}$
8. $\frac{40}{50}$ or $\frac{4}{5}$

Proper Fractions 21

1. $\frac{7}{5}$ or $1\frac{2}{5}$
2. $\frac{7}{7}$ or 1
3. $\frac{10}{8}$ or $1\frac{1}{4}$
4. $\frac{27}{25}$ or $1\frac{2}{25}$
5. $\frac{30}{20}$ or $1\frac{1}{2}$
6. $\frac{16}{9}$ or $1\frac{7}{9}$
7. $\frac{10}{10}$ or $1\frac{3}{5}$
8. $\frac{40}{24}$ or $1\frac{2}{3}$
9. $\frac{18}{15}$ or $1\frac{1}{5}$

$1\frac{7}{9}$	$1\frac{8}{9}$	$1\frac{1}{2}$	$1\frac{1}{5}$	$1\frac{1}{25}$	$1\frac{3}{5}$
NO	AL	TT	HE	WA	ON
$1\frac{1}{4}$	$1\frac{5}{9}$	$1\frac{2}{9}$	$1\frac{2}{5}$	$1\frac{9}{10}$	$1\frac{2}{3}$
LY	YS	LE	SW	SS	ER
$1\frac{7}{10}$	$1\frac{1}{3}$	1	$1\frac{7}{25}$	$1\frac{2}{25}$	$1\frac{1}{6}$
TH	AN	E	TW	OT	O

ALWAYS LESS THAN TWO.

Fraction Subtraction 22

1. $\frac{1}{5}$; fifth; 1
2. $\frac{2}{9}$; ninths; ninths; 2 ninths
3. $\frac{5}{15}$ or $\frac{1}{3}$; 7 fifteenths; 2 fifteenths; 5 fifteenths
4. $\frac{2}{10}$ or $\frac{1}{5}$; 3 tenths; 1 tenth; 2 tenths
5. $\frac{5}{11}$
6. $\frac{4}{20}$ or $\frac{1}{5}$
7. $\frac{6}{25}$
8. $\frac{6}{50}$ or $\frac{3}{25}$

B

0-7682-2636-8 Step-by-Step Fractions

F.Y.I. Concerning LCMs 23
1. 30
2. 28
3. 40
4. 36
5. 30
6. 60
7. 42
8. 54
9. 60
10. 600

Bonus: #10 LCM is 10 times as much as #9, just like the numbers.

Addition: Unlike Denominators 24
1. $\frac{17}{20}$
2. $1\frac{3}{10}$
3. $1\frac{1}{6}$
4. $\frac{11}{14}$
5. $1\frac{19}{24}$
6. $1\frac{11}{36}$
7. $1\frac{11}{50}$
8. $\frac{33}{40}$

Tic-Tac-Toe 25
1. Row 1: $1\frac{3}{4}$
   Row 2: $1\frac{1}{4}$
   Row 3: 2
   Column 1: $1\frac{1}{8}$
   Column 2: $1\frac{7}{8}$
   Column 3: 2
   Diagonal (lower left to upper right): 1 TTT
   Diagonal (upper left to lower right): 2
2. Row 1: $1\frac{1}{2}$
   Row 2: $1\frac{1}{3}$
   Row 3: $1\frac{11}{12}$
   Column 1: $1\frac{1}{4}$
   Column 2: 1 TTT
   Column 3: $2\frac{1}{2}$
   Diagonal (lower left to upper right): $1\frac{7}{12}$
   Diagonal (upper left to lower right): $1\frac{1}{3}$
3. Row 1: $\frac{23}{30}$
   Row 2: $1\frac{19}{30}$
   Row 3: 1 TTT
   Column 1: $1\frac{1}{6}$
   Column 2: $1\frac{1}{5}$
   Column 3: $1\frac{1}{30}$
   Diagonal (lower left to upper right): $1\frac{1}{6}$
   Diagonal (upper left to lower right): $1\frac{1}{5}$

Subtraction: Unlike Denominators 26
1. $\frac{13}{30}$
2. $\frac{11}{40}$
3. $\frac{1}{15}$
4. $\frac{1}{14}$

5. $\frac{19}{40}$
6. $\frac{1}{18}$
7. $\frac{7}{50}$
8. $\frac{9}{40}$

Magic Square Fractions 27

$\frac{1}{6}$	$\frac{1}{8}$	$\frac{1}{3}$
$\frac{3}{8}$	$\frac{5}{24}$	$\frac{1}{24}$
$\frac{1}{12}$	$\frac{7}{24}$	$\frac{1}{4}$

When There Is Too Much or Too Little 28
1. $10\frac{3}{4}$
2. $7\frac{2}{3}$
3. $13\frac{4}{5}$
4. $3\frac{4}{15}$
5. 8
6. 9
7. 3
8. 9; 2
9. $\frac{4}{3}$
10. $\frac{9}{5}$
11. $11\frac{11}{4}$
12. $2\frac{11}{10}$

Addition: Mixed Numbers With
Like Denominators 29
1. $16\frac{5}{7}$
2. $12\frac{2}{3}$
3. $12\frac{2}{5}$
4. $5\frac{5}{11}$
5. $30\frac{3}{5}$
6. $20\frac{1}{5}$
7. $14\frac{2}{3}$
8. $29\frac{2}{5}$

Falling Fractions 30
1. $9\frac{2}{5}$
2. $6\frac{1}{3}$
3. $4\frac{1}{2}$
4. $9\frac{3}{5}$
5. $9\frac{1}{2}$
6. 8
7. $9\frac{5}{11}$
8. $8\frac{1}{5}$
TOP HEAVY

Answer Key

1. $9 \frac{13}{20}$
2. $14 \frac{5}{6}$
3. $12 \frac{29}{40}$
4. $15 \frac{7}{4}$
5. $30 \frac{2}{3}$
6. $25 \frac{2}{3}$

$14 \frac{5}{6}$	$14 \frac{3}{3}$	$25 \frac{2}{3}$	$25 \frac{5}{6}$	$12 \frac{6}{7}$	$12 \frac{29}{40}$
EPL	EDU	ACE	CET	OLO	THE
$30 \frac{5}{6}$	$15 \frac{3}{3}$	$30 \frac{2}{3}$	$9 \frac{4}{5}$	$15 \frac{7}{9}$	$9 \frac{13}{20}$
WES	TTE	TOP	RMS	NUM	BER

REDUCE TO LOWEST TERMS.

1. $11 \frac{6}{35}$
2. $14 \frac{11}{18}$
3. $11 \frac{5}{8}$
4. $8 \frac{11}{50}$
5. $24 \frac{11}{35}$
6. $11 \frac{7}{15}$
7. $11 \frac{11}{16}$

They contain an 11.

1. $2 \frac{4}{7}$
2. $2 \frac{4}{9}$
3. $2 \frac{2}{5}$
4. $1 \frac{5}{11}$
5. $10 \frac{1}{3}$
6. $7 \frac{1}{5}$
7. $5 \frac{4}{7}$
8. $5 \frac{1}{3}$

$2 \frac{2}{5}$	$10 \frac{5}{6}$	$10 \frac{1}{3}$	$5 \frac{2}{7}$	$5 \frac{1}{4}$
TO	AL	OS	RE	AD
$2 \frac{4}{7}$	$2 \frac{4}{9}$	$5 \frac{3}{7}$	$7 \frac{1}{5}$	$1 \frac{1}{5}$
MA	LL	YR	TO	ED
$2 \frac{1}{5}$	$1 \frac{5}{11}$	$5 \frac{4}{7}$	$7 \frac{1}{4}$	$5 \frac{1}{3}$
UC	BE	GI	ED	NS

ALREADY REDUCED

1. $5 \frac{4}{5}$
2. $3 \frac{2}{3}$
3. $3 \frac{3}{4}$
4. $4 \frac{4}{25}$
5. $8 \frac{8}{11}$
6. $2 \frac{2}{3}$
7. $11 \frac{11}{15}$
8. $1 \frac{1}{4}$

They have the same number twice.

1. $2 \frac{3}{20}$
2. $5 \frac{1}{6}$
3. $1 \frac{7}{40}$
4. $4 \frac{5}{9}$
5. $8 \frac{1}{15}$
6. $9 \frac{1}{6}$
7. $6 \frac{7}{12}$

$2 \frac{3}{20}$	$2 \frac{1}{10}$	$9 \frac{5}{6}$	$9 \frac{1}{3}$	$8 \frac{1}{15}$	$1 \frac{7}{40}$	$1 \frac{2}{5}$
OWE	EAS	STM	TCO	ULT	IPL	MMO
$4 \frac{1}{3}$	$8 \frac{1}{5}$	$4 \frac{5}{9}$	$6 \frac{1}{3}$	$5 \frac{1}{6}$	$6 \frac{2}{3}$	$6 \frac{7}{12}$
NDE	NOM	ENE	INA	EDE	TOR	ENT

LEAST COMMON DENOMINATOR

$8 \frac{1}{3}$	$1 \frac{1}{24}$	$6 \frac{1}{4}$
$3 \frac{1}{8}$	$5 \frac{5}{24}$	$7 \frac{7}{24}$
$4 \frac{1}{6}$	$9 \frac{3}{8}$	$2 \frac{1}{12}$

Magic Sum is $15 \frac{5}{8}$.

Column A	Column B
N 1. $3 \frac{1}{4}$	T. $3 \frac{7}{12}$
O 2. $5 \frac{5}{8}$	N. $3 \frac{1}{4}$
I 3. $7 \frac{7}{12}$	C. $4 \frac{1}{3}$
T 4. $3 \frac{7}{12}$	A. $7 \frac{1}{3}$
C 5. $4 \frac{1}{3}$	F. $4 \frac{3}{4}$
A 6. $7 \frac{1}{3}$	I. $7 \frac{7}{12}$
R 7. $4 \frac{1}{4}$	R. $4 \frac{1}{4}$
F 8. $4 \frac{3}{4}$	O. $5 \frac{5}{8}$

FRACTION

$\frac{3}{4}$	$3 \frac{3}{8}$	$1 \frac{1}{2}$
$2 \frac{5}{8}$	$1 \frac{7}{8}$	$1 \frac{1}{8}$
$2 \frac{1}{4}$	$\frac{3}{8}$	3

Magic Sum is $5 \frac{5}{8}$.

	$2 \frac{3}{8}$	−	$1 \frac{7}{8}$	=	$\frac{1}{2}$	
	−				+	
	$\frac{1}{4}$	+	$\frac{1}{2}$	=	$\frac{3}{4}$	
	=		+		=	
$2 \frac{1}{2}$	$2 \frac{1}{8}$	−	$\frac{7}{8}$	=	$1 \frac{1}{4}$	
−			=			
$\frac{5}{8}$	+	$\frac{3}{4}$	=	$1 \frac{3}{8}$		$1 \frac{7}{8}$
=		+				+
$1 \frac{7}{8}$	−	$\frac{7}{8}$	=	1		$1 \frac{1}{4}$
=		=				
$1 \frac{5}{8}$	+	$1 \frac{1}{2}$	=	$3 \frac{1}{8}$		

Answer Key

Working Hard—Time Clock 40
1. $\frac{1}{6}$, $\frac{1}{3}$, $\frac{1}{2}$, $\frac{2}{3}$, $\frac{5}{6}$
2. Alex 27 $\frac{5}{6}$ Amy 29 $\frac{1}{6}$
   Alice 29 $\frac{1}{6}$ Aaron 29 $\frac{1}{2}$
3. Amy; 1 $\frac{1}{3}$ hours
4. Aaron; $\frac{1}{3}$ hours
5. No; $\frac{1}{4}$ hour would be 15 minutes. The time clock records 10-minute intervals.

Modeling Multiplication 41
1. $\frac{1}{8}$
2. $\frac{2}{9}$
3. $\frac{2}{12}$ or $\frac{1}{6}$

Multiplying Fractions 42

$\frac{3}{4}$	x	$\frac{2}{3}$	x	$\frac{4}{5}$	=	$\frac{2}{5}$
		x				
$\frac{2}{15}$		$\frac{6}{7}$		$\frac{2}{25}$		
$\frac{7}{8}$	x	$\frac{4}{4}$	x	$\frac{3}{7}$	=	$\frac{1}{6}$
$\frac{5}{6}$		$\frac{5}{4}$		$\frac{12}{25}$		$\frac{5}{6}$
x				=		x
$\frac{6}{11}$		$\frac{5}{7}$		$\frac{5}{22}$		$\frac{12}{13}$
=				x		x
$\frac{2}{33}$	x	$\frac{3}{8}$	x	$\frac{11}{15}$	=	$\frac{1}{60}$
$\frac{5}{13}$	x	$\frac{1}{6}$	x	$\frac{1}{5}$	=	$\frac{1}{78}$

Multiplying Mixed Numbers 43
1. 6
2. 8 $\frac{2}{5}$
3. 26 $\frac{1}{4}$
4. 9
5. 22 $\frac{6}{7}$
6. 7 $\frac{1}{2}$
7. 51 $\frac{1}{3}$
8. 11 $\frac{3}{7}$
9. 15 $\frac{2}{5}$
10. 6 $\frac{3}{5}$

$8\frac{2}{5}$ S	$14\frac{4}{5}$ I	$15\frac{2}{5}$ M	$25\frac{3}{4}$ S	$26\frac{1}{4}$ A	$22\frac{6}{7}$ D
$11\frac{3}{7}$ D	$50\frac{2}{3}$ P	$51\frac{1}{3}$ L	6 I	$6\frac{1}{2}$ R	$9\frac{1}{3}$ O
$7\frac{2}{3}$ P	$7\frac{1}{2}$ F	$6\frac{3}{5}$ Y	8 E	9 T	$30\frac{1}{7}$ R

IS PROPER

Modeling Division 44
1. 5; 5; 5
2. 6; 6; 6
3. 7; 7; 7
4. $\frac{1}{2}$; $\frac{5}{2}$ or 2 $\frac{1}{2}$
5. 7; 8; 7
multiplication; reciprocal

As Easy As 1, 2, 3—
Dividing Mixed Numbers 45

$2\frac{1}{2}$	÷	$1\frac{2}{3}$	=	$1\frac{1}{2}$
÷				÷
$1\frac{1}{2}$	÷	$\frac{1}{3}$	=	$4\frac{1}{2}$
=		÷		=
$1\frac{2}{3}$	÷	5	=	$\frac{1}{3}$
÷		=		
$1\frac{3}{5}$	÷	24	=	$\frac{1}{15}$	$3\frac{1}{2}$
=		÷		÷
$\frac{5}{6}$	÷	$1\frac{1}{7}$	=	$\frac{35}{48}$	$1\frac{3}{25}$
=				= .
21	÷	$6\frac{18}{25}$	=	$3\frac{1}{8}$

(with left column entries $1\frac{1}{3}$, $1\frac{3}{5}$, $\frac{5}{6}$)

Invert and Multiply 46
Column A   Column B
L 1. 1 $\frac{1}{8}$ P. $\frac{9}{7}$ or 1 $\frac{2}{7}$
A 2. $\frac{9}{10}$ A. $\frac{9}{10}$
C 3. 1 $\frac{3}{4}$ C. 1 $\frac{3}{4}$
O 4. 1 $\frac{2}{9}$ C. $\frac{2}{3}$
R 5. $\frac{9}{20}$ L. 1 $\frac{1}{8}$
P 6. 1 $\frac{2}{7}$ E. 10
I 7. 1 $\frac{1}{3}$ I. 1 $\frac{1}{3}$
C 8. $\frac{2}{3}$ R. 4 $\frac{2}{9}$
E 9. 10   R. $\frac{9}{20}$
R 10. 4 $\frac{2}{9}$ O. 1 $\frac{2}{9}$
RECIPROCAL

Magical Review 47
1 $\frac{3}{4}$	$\frac{1}{8}$	1 $\frac{1}{2}$	$\frac{7}{8}$
1 $\frac{3}{8}$	1	1 $\frac{5}{8}$	1 $\frac{1}{4}$
$\frac{5}{8}$	1 $\frac{1}{4}$	$\frac{3}{8}$	2
$\frac{1}{2}$	1 $\frac{7}{8}$	$\frac{3}{4}$	1 $\frac{1}{8}$

Magic Sum is 4 $\frac{1}{4}$.

Fraction Quiz 48
Corrected Errors
1. $\frac{5}{6}$
2. 1 $\frac{1}{2}$
6. 3 $\frac{1}{2}$
7. $\frac{1}{9}$

© McGraw-Hill Children's Publishing

0-7682-2636-8 *Step-by-Step Fractions*

Answer Key

8. $4\frac{1}{6}$
9. 15
12. 2

Blonde Brownies 49
1. margarine $\frac{2}{3}$ c; brown sugar 2 c; eggs 2; vanilla 2 t; flour 2 c; baking powder 1 t; salt $\frac{1}{4}$ t; chocolate chips 1 c
2. margarine 1 c; brown sugar 3 c; eggs 3; vanilla 3 t; flour 3 c; baking powder $1\frac{1}{2}$ t; salt $\frac{3}{8}$ t; chocolate chips $1\frac{1}{2}$ c
3. margarine $\frac{5}{6}$ c; brown sugar $2\frac{1}{2}$ c; eggs $2\frac{1}{2}$; vanilla $2\frac{1}{2}$ t; flour $2\frac{1}{2}$ c; baking powder $1\frac{1}{4}$ t; salt $\frac{5}{16}$ t; chocolate chips $1\frac{1}{4}$ c

Bonus: 10" x 16"

Under Foot 50
1. Area = 102 sq. ft.
   Carpet = $11\frac{1}{2}$ sq. yd. (rounded up $11\frac{1}{3}$ sq. yd.)
2. Area = $206\frac{1}{4}$ sq. ft.
   Carpet = 23 sq. yd. (rounded up $22\frac{11}{12}$ sq. yd.)
3. Area = 315 sq. ft.
   Carpet = 35 sq. yd.

Decimal Fractions 51
1. 5.2
2. 56.1
3. 45.4
4. 12.75
5. 345.23
6. 72.57
7. 654.322
8. 567.543
9. 45.568
10. 9.3453
11. 65.3891
12. 381.8768

Bonus: $24.57; 4.53, 4.48, 4.54

Fractions→Decimals 52
1. 0.625
2. 0.5
3. 0.6
4. 0.66...
5. 0.09
6. $\frac{1}{8}$
7. $\frac{6}{25}$
8. $\frac{1}{4}$
9. $\frac{7}{8}$
10. $\frac{9}{10}$

$\frac{1}{8}$ ITK	0.625 ITI	$\frac{2}{8}$ SOS	$\frac{2}{5}$ EPT	$\frac{1}{4}$ SLO
0.6 WTO	$\frac{1}{3}$ REP	0.66... KNO	0.5 WWH	$\frac{1}{5}$ ATT
0.9 EAT	$\frac{6}{25}$ ODO	$\frac{3}{10}$ ALO	0.09 ENT	0.7 ING

IT KEPT REPEATING

More or Less 53
1. <
2. <
3. <
4. >
5. <
6. >
7. >
8. <
9. >
10. >

Bonus: 0.45, $\frac{5}{9}$, 0.6, $\frac{2}{3}$, $\frac{3}{4}$

Tic-Tac-Two 52
1. Row 1: 2 TTT
   Row 2: 1.7
   Row 3: 1.7
   Column 1: 1.4
   Column 2: 1.5
   Column 3: 2.5
   Diagonal (lower left to upper right): 2.4
   Diagonal (upper left to lower right): 2.5
2. Row 1: 2.31
   Row 2: 2.01
   Row 3: 1.48
   Column 1: 2.2
   Column 2: 2 TTT
   Column 3: 1.6
   Diagonal (lower left to upper right): 1.55
   Diagonal (upper left to lower right): 3.57
3. Row 1: 2.05
   Row 2: 2.05
   Row 3: 2.01
   Column 1: 2.22
   Column 2: 1.9
   Column 3: 1.99
   Diagonal (lower left to upper right): 3.01
   Diagonal (upper left to lower right): 2 TTT

Decimal Drill: Subtraction 55
1. 0.7
2. 6.59
3. 8.46
4. 29.08
5. 8.11
6. 10.5
7. 1.14
8. 4.413
9. 4.55
10. 5.709

8.11 S	5.711 T	0.7 D	5.709 M	4.65 O	4.55 P
4.413 N	29.08 O	9.54 L	10.5 T	4.387 I	8.46 K
2.14 N	1.14 A	1.7 E	11.5 U	6.59 N	29.12 P

TO LINE UP

0-7682-2636-8 *Step-by-Step Fractions*

Answer Key

Border Patrol 56
1. 12.7 m; 2.3 m
2. 11.65 m
3. 58.7 ft.; 55.5 ft.
4. 36.75 in.; 110.25 in.

Multiplication Maze 57

	0.25	x	6.4	=	1.6
	x				x
	4.4	x	0.55	=	2.42
	=		x		=
0.35	1.1	x	3.52	=	3.872
x					
1.1	x	1.76	=	1.936	6.6
=		x			x
0.385	x	24	=	9.24	4.8
		=			
	42.24	x	0.75	=	31.68

A Pirate's Problem: Decimal Division 58
1. 3.14
2. 7.05
3. 9.8
4. 23.4
5. 3.6
6. 65
7. 9.6
8. 1.369
9. 8.8
10. 0.8

96	9.6	0.8	9.8	1.369
PO	IM	SO	SA	DI
8.8	23.4	6.5	65	7.5
DO	NO	LL	T	YG
3.6	0.36	3.14	8	7.05
KE	ON	SI	E!	TI

POLLY GONE (polygon)

Weighing In 59
1. 2.8 kilograms; 6.16 pounds; yes
2. 7.7 pounds
3. 156.25 grams
4. 6.25 grams
5. 2.5 grams

By the Foot.. 60
1. $200
2. $199
3. $85
4. $164.50 (Must buy 14' of carpet because it is only 12' wide.)
Bonus: $105.75 (Only need 9' of carpet 15' wide.)

Decimal Chains.. 61
1. 1.51 → 7.55 → 7.5 → 9
2. 0.35 → 0.5 → 0.75 → 0.6
3. 0.25 → 0.6 → 0.4 → 0.9
4. 0.275 → 0.195 → 1.95 → 3
Bonus: 9 → 5.4 → 4.5 → 7.5

Multiplication Towers 62

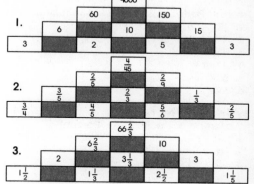

1.

	9000		
	60	150	
6	10	15	
3	2	5	3

2.

	$\frac{4}{45}$		
	$\frac{2}{5}$	$\frac{2}{9}$	
$\frac{3}{5}$	$\frac{2}{3}$	$\frac{1}{3}$	
$\frac{3}{4}$	$\frac{4}{5}$	$\frac{5}{6}$	$\frac{2}{5}$

3.

	$66\frac{2}{3}$		
	$6\frac{2}{3}$	10	
2	$3\frac{1}{3}$	3	
$1\frac{1}{2}$	$1\frac{1}{3}$	$2\frac{1}{2}$	$1\frac{1}{5}$

4.

	0.0144		
	0.12	0.12	
0.6	0.2	0.6	
1.2	0.5	0.4	1.5

Ratios.. 63
1. A. $\frac{18}{12}$ or $\frac{3}{2}$ C. $\frac{18}{30}$ or $\frac{3}{5}$
   B. $\frac{12}{18}$ or $\frac{2}{3}$ D. $\frac{30}{12}$ or $\frac{5}{2}$
2. A. $\frac{5}{6}$ C. $\frac{3}{4}$
   B. $\frac{5}{4}$ D. $\frac{6}{18}$ or $\frac{1}{3}$
                                          E. $\frac{18}{3}$ or $\frac{6}{1}$
3. A. $\frac{13}{52}$ or $\frac{1}{4}$ C. $\frac{4}{52}$ or $\frac{1}{13}$
   B. $\frac{13}{13}$ or $\frac{1}{1}$ D. $\frac{12}{52}$ or $\frac{3}{13}$

Measure for Measure 64
1. $\frac{1}{3}$
2. $\frac{1}{4}$
3. $\frac{1}{5}$
4. $\frac{3}{4}$
5. $\frac{7}{10}$
6. $\frac{3}{8}$
7. $\frac{5}{8}$
8. $\frac{1}{8}$
9. $\frac{1}{20}$
10. $\frac{2}{5}$

$\frac{3}{5}$	$\frac{1}{8}$	$\frac{7}{8}$	$\frac{1}{10}$	$\frac{1}{5}$	$\frac{3}{10}$	$\frac{7}{20}$
C	U	H	A	R	R	L
$\frac{3}{20}$	$\frac{2}{5}$	$\frac{11}{20}$	$\frac{1}{35}$	$\frac{3}{8}$	$\frac{1}{4}$	$\frac{1}{9}$
E	U	M	A	S	C	G
$\frac{1}{20}$	$\frac{2}{9}$	$\frac{1}{3}$	$\frac{5}{8}$	$\frac{3}{4}$	$\frac{8}{9}$	$\frac{7}{10}$
A	N	S	E	R	E	T

CHARLEMAGNE

Answer Key

Proportions **65**
1. A = 7
2. B = 3
3. C = 15
4. D = 36
5. E = 21
6. F = 12

One possible answer: $\frac{4}{8} = \frac{9}{18}$; both = $\frac{1}{2}$

Percent Parts **66**
1. 12 hearts shaded
2. 9 stars
3. 4 diamonds
4. 2 arrows
5. 60%
6. 64%

By Any Other Name **67**

Fraction	Decimal	Percent
1. $\frac{2}{5}$	0.4	40%
2. $\frac{13}{20}$	0.65	65%
3. $\frac{1}{5}$	0.2	20%
4. $\frac{1}{3}$	0.333…	33.3…%
5. $\frac{9}{10}$	0.9	90%
6. $\frac{3}{20}$	0.15	15%
7. $\frac{7}{8}$	0.875	87.5%
8. $\frac{1}{4}$	0.25	25%
9. $\frac{1}{25}$	0.04	4%

Bonus: 45.6%; 0.036

Percent Count **68**
1. Red /: 81, 82, 83, …, 100   20%
2. Blue /: 2, 4, 6, 8, 10, 12, …, 100   50%
3. Green |:5, 10, 15, 20, 25, …, 100   20%
4. Yellow —: 1, 2, 3, 4, 6, 8, 9, 12, 18, 24, 36, 72   12%
5. Black x: 1, 2, 3, 4, …, 10   10%

Bonus: 2% (numbers 90 and 100)

PARTing Shots **69**
1. 20%
2. 90%
3. 33 1/3%
4. 75%
5. 25%

Math : English = Proportion : Analogy **70**
1. day
2. yard
3. inch
4. month
5. yard
6. 10
7. 26
8. 60
9. 10
10. 360

Bonus: Answers will vary. Sample answers:
11. 1 : 50 = state : United States
12. 1 : 4 = quarter : dollar

Tips **71**
1. $4.80
2. $6.40
3. $1.80 + $0.90 = $2.70
4. $2.44 + $1.22 = $3.66
5. $3.60 → $7.20

Fraction Scramble **72**
1. improper
2. greatest
3. lowest
4. percent
5. one
6. five
7. reciprocals
8. least
9. three
10. ratio
11. mixed
12. numerator

H

0-7682-2636-8 *Step-by-Step Fractions*

Name_____ Date _____

Sums and Differences

Match each sum in Column A to an equal difference in Column B.

Column A

_____ 1. $1\frac{1}{2} + 1\frac{3}{4}$

_____ 2. $3\frac{3}{16} + 2\frac{7}{16}$

_____ 3. $4\frac{1}{3} + 3\frac{1}{4}$

_____ 4. $1\frac{5}{6} + 1\frac{3}{4}$

_____ 5. $2\frac{2}{3} + 1\frac{2}{3}$

_____ 6. $1\frac{5}{6} + 5\frac{1}{2}$

_____ 7. $2\frac{1}{12} + 2\frac{1}{6}$

_____ 8. $2\frac{1}{2} + 2\frac{1}{4}$

Column B

T. $5\frac{2}{3} - 2\frac{1}{12}$

N. $6 - 2\frac{3}{4}$

C. $9\frac{2}{3} - 5\frac{1}{3}$

A. $8\frac{1}{6} - \frac{5}{6}$

F. $8\frac{1}{2} - 3\frac{3}{4}$

I. $10\frac{1}{3} - 2\frac{3}{4}$

R. $7\frac{1}{8} - 2\frac{7}{8}$

O. $8\frac{1}{4} - 2\frac{5}{8}$

Check it! Write the Column A match letters from bottom to top:

___ ___ ___ ___ ___ ___ ___ ___

37

0-7682-2636-8 *Step-by-Step Fractions*

Magical Fractions

In a Magic Square, each row, column, and diagonal has the same sum. Complete the problems and determine the Magic Sum.

$2\frac{1}{4} - 1\frac{1}{2}$	$1\frac{1}{2} + 1\frac{7}{8}$	$4\frac{1}{8} - 2\frac{5}{8}$
$1\frac{1}{2} + 1\frac{1}{8}$	$5\frac{3}{8} - 3\frac{1}{2}$	$\frac{3}{8} + \frac{3}{4}$
$1\frac{5}{8} + \frac{5}{8}$	$7\frac{1}{4} - 6\frac{7}{8}$	$1\frac{7}{8} + 1\frac{1}{8}$

The Magic Sum is _____.

0-7682-2636-8 *Step-by-Step Fractions*

Name_____ Date _____

Fraction Maze

Fill in the blanks so the fraction sentences are true.

$2\frac{3}{8}$	—	$1\frac{7}{8}$	=	
—				+
	+	$\frac{1}{2}$	=	$\frac{3}{4}$
=		+		=
$2\frac{1}{8}$	—	$\frac{7}{8}$	=	
		=		
$\frac{5}{8}$	+		=		
=		+			+
$1\frac{7}{8}$	—	$\frac{7}{8}$	=		$1\frac{1}{4}$
		=			=
	$1\frac{5}{8}$	+		=	$3\frac{1}{8}$

© McGraw-Hill Children's Publishing

0-7682-2636-8 *Step-by-Step Fractions*

Name_____ Date _____

Working Hard—Time Clock

The time clock at Acme Company records time in 10-minute intervals.

Employee Time Report in Hours

Name	M	T	W	T	F
Alex	$7\frac{1}{2}$	$6\frac{5}{6}$	$4\frac{1}{3}$	$5\frac{2}{3}$	$3\frac{1}{2}$
Amy	$7\frac{1}{3}$	$8\frac{1}{6}$	$3\frac{1}{2}$	$5\frac{5}{6}$	$4\frac{1}{3}$
Alice	$6\frac{1}{2}$	$7\frac{2}{3}$	$5\frac{1}{6}$	$4\frac{1}{2}$	$5\frac{1}{3}$
Aaron	7	$6\frac{2}{3}$	$4\frac{1}{2}$	$6\frac{1}{2}$	$4\frac{5}{6}$

1. What fraction of an hour is 10 minutes? _____

   20 minutes?_____ 30 minutes? _____

   40 minutes? _____50 minutes?_____

2. How many hours did each employee work during the week?

   Alex _____   Amy _____

   Alice _____   Aaron _____

3. Did Alex or Amy work longer?_____

   How much longer? _____

4. Did Alice or Aaron work longer? _____

   How much longer? _____

5. Will the time report ever show $5\frac{1}{4}$ hours?_____

   If no, why not?_____

40

© McGraw-Hill Children's Publishing

0-7682-2636-8 *Step-by-Step Fractions*

Modeling Multiplication

Example: Fold a piece of paper in thirds and shade $\frac{1}{2}$ of one of the thirds. How much of the paper is shaded? $\frac{1}{6}$

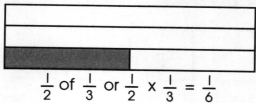

$\frac{1}{2}$ of $\frac{1}{3}$ or $\frac{1}{2} \times \frac{1}{3} = \frac{1}{6}$

1. Fold a piece of paper in half. Shade $\frac{1}{4}$ of one of the halves. How much of the paper is shaded? _____

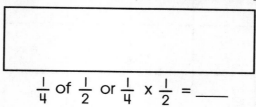

$\frac{1}{4}$ of $\frac{1}{2}$ or $\frac{1}{4} \times \frac{1}{2} =$ ____

2. Fold a piece of paper into thirds. Shade $\frac{2}{3}$ of one of the thirds. How much of the paper is shaded? _____

$\frac{2}{3}$ of $\frac{1}{3}$ or $\frac{2}{3} \times \frac{1}{3} =$ ____

3. Fold a piece of paper into fourths. Shade $\frac{2}{3}$ of one of the fourths. How much of the paper is shaded? _____

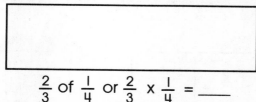

$\frac{2}{3}$ of $\frac{1}{4}$ or $\frac{2}{3} \times \frac{1}{4} =$ ____

41

Multiplying Fractions

Multiply numerators and multiply denominators.

Example: $\dfrac{3}{4} \times \dfrac{2}{5} \times \dfrac{1}{3} = \dfrac{(3 \times 2 \times 1)}{(4 \times 5 \times 3)} = \dfrac{6}{60}$ or $\dfrac{1}{10}$

$\dfrac{3}{4}$	x	$\dfrac{2}{3}$	x	$\dfrac{4}{5}$	=	
		x				
$\dfrac{2}{15}$		$\dfrac{6}{7}$				
$\dfrac{7}{8}$	x	$\dfrac{4}{9}$	x	$\dfrac{3}{7}$	=	
$\dfrac{5}{6}$		$\dfrac{5}{4}$		$\dfrac{12}{25}$		$\dfrac{5}{6}$
x		=		x		x
$\dfrac{6}{11}$				$\dfrac{5}{22}$		$\dfrac{12}{13}$
=				x		x
	x	$\dfrac{3}{8}$	x	$\dfrac{11}{15}$	=	
						=
$\dfrac{5}{13}$	x	$\dfrac{1}{6}$	x	$\dfrac{1}{5}$	=	

0-7682-2636-8 *Step-by-Step Fractions*

Multiplying Mixed Numbers

Write mixed numbers as improper fractions and then multiply.

Example: $4\frac{2}{3} \times 3\frac{1}{2} = \frac{14}{3} \times \frac{7}{2} = \frac{98}{6} = 16\frac{2}{6}$ or $16\frac{1}{3}$

Solve each problem. Cross out the answers below. Use the remaining letters to complete the statement.

1. $2\frac{2}{3} \times 2\frac{1}{4}$

2. $3\frac{1}{5} \times 2\frac{5}{8}$

3. $6\frac{1}{8} \times 4\frac{2}{7}$

4. $5\frac{2}{5} \times 1\frac{2}{3}$

5. $10\frac{5}{7} \times 2\frac{2}{15}$

6. $7\frac{1}{7} \times 1\frac{1}{20}$

7. $8\frac{4}{5} \times 5\frac{5}{6}$

8. $6\frac{2}{3} \times 1\frac{5}{7}$

9. $4\frac{2}{5} \times 3\frac{1}{2}$

10. $2\frac{3}{4} \times 2\frac{2}{5}$

$8\frac{2}{5}$	$14\frac{4}{5}$	$15\frac{2}{5}$	$25\frac{3}{4}$	$26\frac{1}{4}$	$22\frac{6}{7}$
S	I	M	S	A	D
$11\frac{3}{7}$	$50\frac{2}{3}$	$51\frac{1}{3}$	6	$6\frac{1}{2}$	$9\frac{1}{3}$
D	P	L	I	R	O
$7\frac{2}{3}$	$7\frac{1}{2}$	$6\frac{3}{5}$	8	9	$30\frac{1}{7}$
P	F	Y	E	T	R

Improper fractions $\frac{4}{3}$ and $\frac{5}{3}$ are polite to $\frac{2}{3}$ because it

___ ___   ___ ___ ___ ___ ___ ___.

43

0-7682-2636-8 *Step-by-Step Fractions*

Modeling Division

Example: How many quarters are in $0.75?

$$\frac{3}{4} \div \frac{1}{4} = 3 \quad \textbf{Notice:} \frac{3}{4} \times 4 = 3$$

Numbers like $\frac{1}{4}$ and $\frac{4}{1}$ are reciprocals.

Fill in the blanks.

1. How many quarters are in $1.25? ____

   $\frac{5}{4} \div \frac{1}{4} =$ ____ **Notice:** $\frac{5}{4} \times 4 =$ ____

2. How many dimes are in $0.60? ____

   $\frac{6}{10} \div \frac{1}{10} =$ ____ **Notice:** $\frac{6}{10} \times 10 =$ ____

3. How many half-dollars are in $3.50? ____

   $\frac{7}{2} \div \frac{1}{2} =$ ____ **Notice:** $\frac{7}{2} \times 2 =$ ____

4. How many half-dollars are in $1.25? ____

   $\frac{5}{4} \div$ ____ $= 2\frac{1}{2}$ **Notice:** $\frac{5}{4} \times 2 =$ ____

Use the pattern.

5. $\frac{7}{8} \div \frac{1}{8} =$ ____ **Notice:** $\frac{7}{8} \times$ ____ $=$ ____

   To divide by a fraction, change the division to

   _____ and use the _____ of the divisor

   (the second fraction).

Remember: To divide by a fraction, invert it and multiply.

44

Name_____ Date _____

As Easy As 1, 2, 3—
Dividing Mixed Numbers

Easy Steps! 1. Write numbers as improper fractions.

2. Change division to multiplication and invert divisor.

3. Multiply and simplify.

$2\frac{1}{2}$	÷	$1\frac{2}{3}$	=	
÷				÷
$1\frac{1}{2}$	÷	$\frac{1}{3}$	=	
=		÷		=
		÷	5	=

$1\frac{1}{3}$			=	
÷				$3\frac{1}{2}$
$1\frac{3}{5}$	÷	24	=	÷
=		÷		
	÷	$1\frac{1}{7}$	=	$1\frac{3}{25}$
		=		=
	÷	$6\frac{18}{25}$	=	

45

0-7682-2636-8 *Step-by-Step Fractions*

Invert and Multiply

Each division problem in Column A is equivalent to a multiplication problem in Column B. Solve each problem and find the matches.

Column A

_____ 1. $\frac{3}{4} \div \frac{2}{3} =$ _____

_____ 2. $\frac{4}{5} \div \frac{8}{9} =$ _____

_____ 3. $\frac{7}{8} \div \frac{1}{2} =$ _____

_____ 4. $\frac{11}{15} \div \frac{3}{5} =$ _____

_____ 5. $\frac{3}{10} \div \frac{2}{3} =$ _____

_____ 6. $1\frac{1}{2} \div 1\frac{1}{6} =$ _____

_____ 7. $3\frac{5}{9} \div 2\frac{2}{3} =$ _____

_____ 8. $4\frac{4}{5} \div 7\frac{1}{5} =$ _____

_____ 9. $6\frac{2}{3} \div \frac{2}{3} =$ _____

_____ 10. $8\frac{4}{9} \div 2 =$ _____

Column B

P. $\frac{3}{2} \times \frac{6}{7}$

A. $\frac{4}{5} \times \frac{9}{8}$

C. $\frac{7}{8} \times \frac{2}{1}$

C. $\frac{24}{5} \times \frac{5}{36}$

L. $\frac{3}{4} \times \frac{3}{2}$

E. $\frac{20}{3} \times \frac{3}{2}$

I. $\frac{32}{9} \times \frac{3}{8}$

R. $\frac{76}{9} \times \frac{1}{2}$

R. $\frac{3}{10} \times \frac{3}{2}$

O. $\frac{11}{15} \times \frac{5}{3}$

Check it! Write the Column A match letters from bottom to top.

___ ___ ___ ___ ___ ___ ___ ___ ___ ___

Magical Review

The sum of each row, column, and diagonal of a Magic Square is the same number—the Magic Sum.

Solve the problems and find the Magic Sum.

$\frac{7}{8} + \frac{7}{8}$	$\frac{1}{2} \times \frac{1}{4}$	$2 \times \frac{3}{4}$	$\frac{1}{2} + \frac{3}{8}$
$\frac{5}{8} + \frac{3}{4}$	$\frac{3}{4} \div \frac{3}{4}$	$\frac{3}{4} + \frac{7}{8}$	$\frac{1}{2} \times \frac{1}{2}$
$\frac{7}{8} - \frac{1}{4}$	$\frac{3}{4} + \frac{1}{2}$	$\frac{3}{4} \div 2$	$\frac{2}{3} \div \frac{1}{3}$
$\frac{3}{4} - \frac{1}{4}$	$2 - \frac{1}{8}$	$\frac{3}{8} + \frac{3}{8}$	$\frac{7}{8} + \frac{1}{4}$

The Magic Sum is _____.

0-7682-2636-8 *Step-by-Step Fractions*

Fraction Quiz

Mattie Matics was confused when she took this quiz. Find and correct the 7 errors Mattie made.

QUIZ: Fraction Operations	**Name:** Mattie Matics
1. $\frac{1}{2} + \frac{1}{3} = \frac{2}{5}$	7. $\frac{1}{3} \times \frac{1}{3} = \frac{1}{6}$
2. $\frac{3}{4} + \frac{3}{4} = \frac{6}{8}$	8. $1\frac{2}{3} \times 2\frac{1}{2} = 2\frac{1}{3}$
3. $2\frac{1}{2} + 3\frac{1}{2} = 6$	9. $4\frac{1}{2} \times 3\frac{1}{3} = 12\frac{1}{6}$
4. $\frac{7}{8} - \frac{2}{3} = \frac{5}{24}$	10. $\frac{3}{4} \div \frac{1}{2} = 1\frac{1}{2}$
5. $2\frac{4}{5} - 1\frac{2}{3} = 1\frac{2}{15}$	11. $\frac{2}{3} \div \frac{3}{4} = \frac{8}{9}$
6. $6\frac{1}{4} - 2\frac{3}{4} = 4\frac{1}{2}$	12. $2\frac{4}{5} \div 1\frac{2}{5} = 2\frac{2}{5}$

48

Blonde Brownies

Blonde Brownies	
$\frac{1}{3}$ c margarine	Preheat oven to 350°F. Mix margarine
1 c brown sugar	and brown sugar together. Add egg and
1 egg, slightly beaten	vanilla. Sift dry ingredients and add to
1 t vanilla	egg mixture. Pour into a greased 8" x 8" pan.
1 c flour	Sprinkle $\frac{1}{2}$c chocolate
$\frac{1}{2}$ t baking powder	chips over the top. Bake for 20–25
$\frac{1}{8}$ t salt	minutes.
$\frac{1}{2}$ c chocolate chips	YIELD: Sixteen 2" x 2" squares

1. Debbie wants to make a double batch. How much of each
   ingredient will be needed? margarine _____
   brown sugar _____ eggs_____ vanilla _____ flour _____
   baking powder_____ salt_____chocolate chips_____

2. Terry wants to triple the recipe. How much of each
   ingredient will be needed? margarine _____
   brown sugar _____ eggs_____ vanilla _____ flour _____
   baking powder_____ salt_____chocolate chips_____

3. Frank wants to make forty 2" x 2" squares. How much of
   each ingredient will be needed? margarine _____
   brown sugar _____ eggs_____vanilla _____ flour_____
   baking powder_____ salt_____chocolate chips_____

Bonus: What size pan might Frank use? _____

49

       0-7682-2636-8 *Step-by-Step Fractions*

Under Foot

Carpet is often sold by the square yard. Rooms are usually measured in feet. Find the area of each floor plan. Convert the area into square yards to determine the amount of carpet needed. Round up to the nearest $\frac{1}{2}$ sq. yd.

Math Hints: $\text{Area}_{rectangle} = L \times W$

9 sq. ft. $= 1$ sq. yd. or 1 sq. ft. $= \frac{1}{9}$ sq. yd.

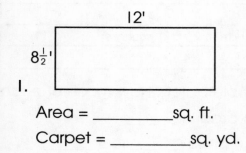

1.

Area = _____ sq. ft.

Carpet = _____ sq. yd.

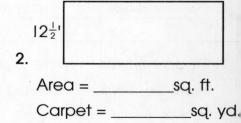

2.

Area = _____ sq. ft.

Carpet = _____ sq. yd.

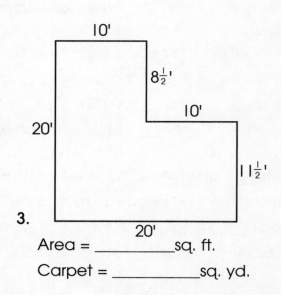

3.

Area = _____ sq. ft.

Carpet = _____ sq. yd.

© McGraw-Hill Children's Publishing

0-7682-2636-8 *Step-by-Step Fractions*

Decimal Fractions

Math Hint: Fractions with denominators of 10, 100, 1000, etc.,
are *decimal fractions*: $\frac{7}{10} = 0.7$; $\frac{23}{100} = 0.23$.

In **12.34567**   3 is in the tenths place
4 is in the hundredths place
5 is in the thousandths place
6 is in the ten-thousandths place
7 is in the hundred-thousandths place

Round to the nearest tenth (12.34567 → 12.3).

1. 5.201   2. 56.124   3. 45.37

Round to the nearest hundredth (12.34567 → 12.35).

4. 12.7531   5. 345.2319   6. 72.5678

Round to the nearest thousandth (12.34567 → 12.346).

7. 654.32211   8. 567.54321   9. 45.5679

Round to the nearest ten-thousandth (12.34567 → 12.3457).

10. 9.34531   11. 65.38912   12. 381.876789

Bonus:
Round to the nearest cent: $24.567 _____

If an object must be 4.5" long to the nearest 0.1", which
measures would be acceptable?

4.43   4.53   4.48   4.54   4.57

51

Fractions → Decimals

Math Hints:

Fractions → Decimals: Divide the numerator by the
    denominator. $\frac{3}{8} = 3 \div 8 = 0.375$

Decimals → Fractions: Write the decimal part over the power
    of ten of the last digit place value. $0.48 = \frac{48}{100} = \frac{12}{25}$

Find the decimal or fraction equivalent. Cross out the answers
below. Use the remaining letters to complete the statement.

1. $\frac{5}{8}$ = _____

2. $\frac{1}{2}$ = _____

3. $\frac{3}{5}$ = _____

4. $\frac{2}{3}$ = _____

5. $\frac{9}{100}$ = _____

6. 0.2 = _____

7. 0.24 = _____

8. 0.25 = _____

9. 0.875 = _____

10. 0.9 = _____

$\frac{1}{8}$	0.625	$\frac{7}{8}$	$\frac{2}{5}$	$\frac{1}{4}$
ITK	ITI	SOS	EPT	SLO
0.6	$\frac{1}{3}$	0.66...	0.5	$\frac{1}{5}$
WTO	REP	KNO	WWH	ATT
0.9	$\frac{6}{25}$	$\frac{9}{10}$	0.09	0.7
EAT	ODO	ALO	ENT	ING

0.75 got tired of listening to $\frac{2}{3}$ talk because

__ __ __ __ __ __ __ __ __ __ __ __ __ __ __ __!

52

0-7682-2636-8 *Step-by-Step Fractions*

Name______________________________ Date ______________

More or Less

Math Hint: Three ways to compare fractions:

1. Use a common denominator and compare the numerators.

   $\frac{1}{2}$? $\frac{1}{3}$

   $\frac{3}{6} > \frac{2}{6}$ so $\frac{1}{2} > \frac{1}{3}$

2. Compare the product of the extremes and the means.

   $\frac{2}{3}$? $\frac{5}{6}$ product of extremes $2 \times 6 = 12$

   product of means $3 \times 5 = 15$ so $\frac{2}{3} < \frac{5}{6}$

3. Write fractions as decimals and compare.

   $\frac{3}{4}$? $\frac{5}{6}$ ➝ $0.75 < 0.83\ldots$ so $\frac{3}{4} < \frac{5}{6}$

Replace the ? with < or >.

1. $\frac{1}{3}$? $\frac{2}{5}$
2. $\frac{4}{7}$? $\frac{5}{8}$
3. $\frac{7}{10}$? $\frac{3}{4}$
4. $\frac{3}{11}$? $\frac{5}{22}$
5. $\frac{2}{9}$? $\frac{2}{7}$
6. $\frac{9}{14}$? $\frac{15}{28}$
7. $\frac{7}{8}$? $\frac{6}{7}$
8. $\frac{3}{5}$? 0.65
9. 0.45 ? $\frac{3}{7}$
10. $\frac{7}{9}$? 0.75

Bonus: Write in order from least to greatest: $\frac{2}{3}$, 0.6, $\frac{3}{4}$, 0.45, $\frac{5}{9}$

____

0-7682-2636-8 *Step-by-Step Fractions*

Tic-Tac-Two

Find the sum of each row, column, and diagonal. Circle the row, column, or diagonal that has a sum of 2 for the Tic-Tac-Two. Remember, add tenths to tenths, hundredths to hundredths, etc.

1.

0.7	0.4	0.9	___
0.1	0.9	0.7	___
0.6	0.2	0.9	___

___   ___   ___

Tic

Tac

2.

1.56	0.65	0.1	___
0.3	1.11	0.6	___
0.34	0.24	0.9	___

___   ___   ___

3.

0.34	0.45	1.26	___
1.08	0.95	0.02	___
0.8	0.5	0.71	___

___   ___   ___

Two

54

© McGraw-Hill Children's Publishing   0-7682-2636-8 *Step-by-Step Fractions*

Decimal Drill: Subtraction

Solve the problems. Cross out the answers below. Use the remaining letters to complete the statement.

1.
```
   2.5
 - 1.8
```

6.
```
   76.2
 - 65.7
```

2.
```
   23.98
 - 17.39
```

7.
```
   5.12
 - 3.98
```

3.
```
   14.25
 - 5.79
```

8.
```
   9.213
 - 4.8
```

4.
```
   56.97
 - 27.89
```

9.
```
   12.1
 - 7.55
```

5.
```
   12.73
 - 4.62
```

10.
```
   7.82
 - 2.111
```

8.11	5.711	0.7	5.709	4.65	4.55
S	T	D	M	O	P
4.413	29.08	9.54	10.5	4.387	8.46
N	O	L	T	I	K
2.14	1.14	1.7	11.5	6.59	29.12
N	A	E	U	N	P

The drill sergeant ordered the problem decimal points,

"__ __   __ __ __ __   __ __!"

55

Border Patrol

Math Hint: Perimeter$_{rectangle}$ = 2(length) + 2(width)

1. Katie wants to have a wallpaper border around her bedroom. The rectangular room measures 3.1 m x 3.25 m. What length of wallpaper border does she need? _____ If she buys 15 m of border, how much extra will she have?

   _____

2. Alex wants to put a chair rail along three walls of the dining room. If the walls measure 3.7 m, 4.25 m, and 3.7 m, what total length of chair rail does he need? _____

3. If a garden measures 12.5' x 16.85', how much fencing would be needed to surround the garden? _____ If a gate measures 3.2', how much fencing must be bought?

   _____

4. Casey is buying ribbon for presents. The bow uses 20.5". The box is 3.25" tall and 4.5" across. The ribbon will go around the box once with a bow on top. Assuming the ribbon will overlap 0.75", how much ribbon must be bought for 1 present? _____ 3 presents? _____

56

Multiplication Maze

Complete each decimal problem.

	0.25	x	6.4	=	
	x				x
	4.4	x	0.55	=	
	=		x		=
0.35		x	3.52	=	3.872
x				=	
1.1	x	1.76	=		6.6
=		x			x
	x	24	=		4.8
		=			=
		x	0.75	=	

57

0-7682-2636-8 *Step-by-Step Fractions*

A Pirate's Problem: Decimal Division

Solve the problems. Cross out the answers. Answer the question at the bottom of the page with the remaining letters.

1. $2.198 \div 0.7 =$

2. $8.46 \div 1.2 =$

3. $49.98 \div 5.1 =$

4. $3.276 \div 0.14 =$

5. $9.108 \div 2.53 =$

6. $18.85 \div 0.29 =$

7. $3.552 \div 0.37 =$

8. $4.107 \div 3 =$

9. $3.3 \div 0.375 =$

10. $7 \div 8.75 =$

96	9.6	0.8	9.8	1.369
PO	IM	SO	SA	DI
8.8	23.4	6.5	65	7.5
DO	NO	LL	T	YG
3.6	0.36	3.14	8	7.05
KE	ON	S!	E!	T!

What did the mathematical pirate say when his parrot left?

__ __ __ __ __   __ __ __ __ __ __

0-7682-2636-8 Step-by-Step Fractions

Name_____ Date _____

Weighing In

Math Fact: I kilogram = 2.2 pounds

1. Terry set a goal of losing 5 pounds over
   the summer. In June, the scale at the fitness
   center read 63.2 kilograms. At the end of August,
   the scale read 60.4 kilograms. How many
   kilograms did he lose? _____ How many
   pounds did he lose? _____ Did he reach
   his goal? _____

2. Ali was concerned when she heard the baby weighed 3.5.
   Then she realized the weight was in kilograms. What was
   the baby's weight in pounds? _____

3. If a penny weighs 3.125 grams, how much does a roll of 50
   pennies weigh (without the wrapper)? _____

4. A roll of quarters ($10.00 worth) weighs 250 grams (without
   the wrapper). How much does I quarter weigh? _____

5. A dime weighs half as much as a nickel. If a roll of nickels
   ($2.00 worth) weighs 200 grams, how much does a dime
   weigh? _____ **Hint:** Find the weight of one nickel first.

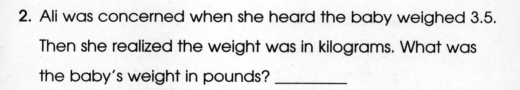

59

Name_____ Date _____

By the Foot

Carpet is often sold by the foot from a roll of carpet 12 feet wide. Calculate the lowest price of carpet for each floor plan. Assume the carpet will be in one piece.

1. 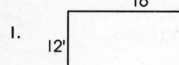 $12.50 per foot Cost: _____

2. 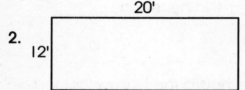 $9.95 per foot   Cost: _____

3. 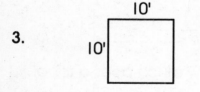 $8.50 per foot   Cost: _____

4. 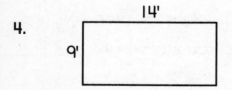 $11.75 per foot Cost: _____

Bonus: If the roll of carpet is 15 feet wide, what would be the lowest cost to carpet floor plan #4? _____

0-7682-2636-8 *Step-by-Step Fractions*

Decimal Chains

Complete each chain. Use the answers in each END shape to complete the Bonus problem.

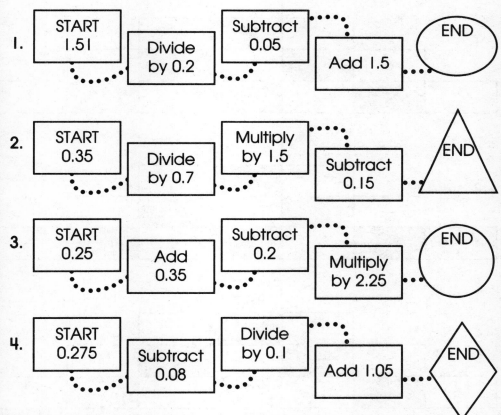

Bonus: Use the END numbers of problems 1-4 to answer the BONUS END.

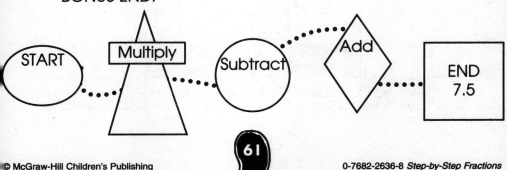

61

0-7682-2636-8 *Step-by-Step Fractions*

Multiplication Towers

Fill in the white boxes to complete each Multiplication Tower.

1.

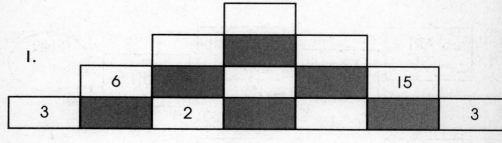

2.

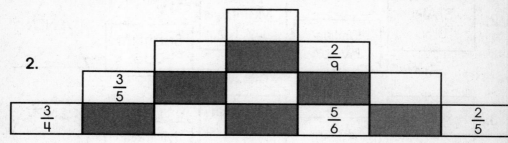

3.

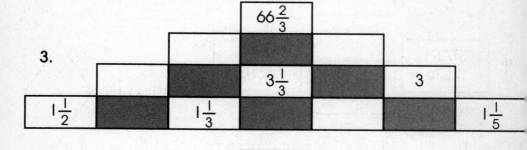

4.

0-7682-2636-8 *Step-by-Step Fractions*

Ratios

A *ratio* is a comparison of 2 quantities. Ratios can be written as fractions.

Example: A class of 24 students has 13 girls.

Ratio of girls to students is $\frac{13}{24}$.

Ratio of girls to boys is $\frac{13}{11}$.

Ratio of students to boys is $\frac{24}{11}$.

Write each ratio. Reduce if possible.

1. A class of 30 students has 18 boys.
   A. Ratio of boys to girls. _____
   B. Ratio of girls to boys. _____
   C. Ratio of boys to students. _____
   D. Ratio of students to girls. _____

2. A bag contains 5 red, 3 green, 4 yellow, and 6 blue marbles.
   A. Ratio of red marbles to blue marbles. _____
   B. Ratio of red marbles to yellow marbles. _____
   C. Ratio of green marbles to yellow marbles. _____
   D. Ratio of blue marbles to all marbles. _____
   E. Ratio of all marbles to green marbles. _____

3. A deck of 52 playing cards (4 suits of 13 cards each).
   A. Ratio of hearts to total cards. _____
   B. Ratio of hearts to diamonds. _____
   C. Ratio of Aces to total cards. _____
   D. Ratio of face cards (Kings, Queens, Jacks)
      to total cards. _____

63

Name_____ Date _____

Measure for Measure

Write each ratio in lowest terms. Cross out the answers and complete the statement with the remaining letters.

Math Hint: The parts of a ratio must have the same unit of measure before reducing. 3 in./1 ft. → 3 in./12 in. → 1/4

1. 1 ft./1 yd. = _____

2. 9 in./1 yd. = _____

3. 12 min./1 hr. = _____

4. 45 min./1 hr. = _____

5. $0.70/$1 = _____

6. 9 in./2 ft. = _____

7. 75 min./2 hr. = _____

8. 30 min./4 hr. = _____

9. 15 sec/5 min. = _____

10. 6 dimes/6 quarters = _____

$\frac{3}{5}$	$\frac{1}{8}$	$\frac{7}{8}$	$\frac{1}{10}$	$\frac{1}{5}$	$\frac{3}{10}$	$\frac{7}{20}$
C	U	H	A	L	R	L
$\frac{3}{20}$	$\frac{2}{5}$	$\frac{11}{20}$	$\frac{1}{35}$	$\frac{3}{8}$	$\frac{1}{4}$	$\frac{1}{9}$
E	U	M	A	S	C	G
$\frac{1}{20}$	$\frac{2}{9}$	$\frac{1}{3}$	$\frac{5}{8}$	$\frac{3}{4}$	$\frac{8}{9}$	$\frac{7}{10}$
A	N	S	E	R	E	T

At one time, the foot was based on the measure of

__ __ __ __ __ __ __ __ __ __ __'s foot.

0-7682-2636-8 *Step-by-Step Fractions*

Proportions

A *proportion* is two equal ratios.

Example: $\frac{6}{8} = \frac{9}{12}$, $\frac{6}{8}$ and $\frac{9}{12}$ both equal $\frac{3}{4}$

Replace the letter with the missing number for each proportion. Cross out each answer in the Answer Bank.

1. $\frac{14}{20} = \frac{A}{10}$

4. $\frac{24}{D} = \frac{20}{30}$

2. $\frac{45}{15} = \frac{9}{B}$

5. $\frac{28}{E} = \frac{20}{15}$

3. $\frac{10}{12} = \frac{C}{18}$

6. $\frac{F}{9} = \frac{16}{12}$

Answer Bank

15	4	21	8
	36	3	18
	12	7	9

Write a proportion using the four remaining numbers:

_____

   0-7682-2636-8 *Step-by-Step Fractions*

Percent Parts

Percent (%) means per hundred.

Example: Shade 60%

$$60\% = \frac{60}{100} \text{ which equals } \frac{3}{5} \text{ or } \frac{9}{15}$$

Shade the items to indicate the given percent.

1. 75% ♡ ♡ ♡ ♡ ♡ ♡ ♡ ♡ ♡ ♡ ♡ ♡ ♡ ♡ ♡ ♡

2. 45% ☆

3. 80% ◊ ◊ ◊ ◊ ◊

4. 10% ⇨

Give the percent of the items shaded in each problem.

5. _____ ♥♥♥♥♥♥♥♥♥♥♥♥♡♡♡♡♡♡♡♡

6. _____ ★ ★ ★ ★ ★ ★ ★ ★ ★ ★ ☆ ☆
    ★ ★ ★ ★ ☆ ☆ ☆ ☆ ☆ ☆ ☆

66

0-7682-2636-8 *Step-by-Step Fractions*

By Any Other Name

Percent means per hundred, hundredths, or 2 decimal places.

Example: $\frac{2}{5} = \frac{4}{100} = 40\%$ or $\frac{2}{5} = 0.40 = 40\%$

$\frac{2}{3} = \frac{66\frac{2}{3}}{100} = 66\frac{2}{3}\%$ or $\frac{2}{3} = 0.666... = 66.6...\%$

Complete the table.

	FRACTION	DECIMAL	PERCENT
1.	$\frac{2}{5}$		
2.		0.65	
3.			20%
4.	$\frac{1}{3}$		
5.		0.9	
6.			15%
7.	$\frac{7}{8}$		
8.		0.25	
9.			4%

Bonus: If the decimal form has 3 decimal places, the percent form will have 1 decimal place:

$$0.375 = \frac{375}{1000} = 37.5\%.$$

$0.456 =$ _____ %   _____ $= 3.6\%$

67

Percent Count

1	2	3	4	5	6	7	8	9	10
11	12	13	14	15	16	17	18	19	20
21	22	23	24	25	26	27	28	29	30
31	32	33	34	35	36	37	38	39	40
41	42	43	44	45	46	47	48	49	50
51	52	53	54	55	56	57	58	59	60
61	62	63	64	65	66	67	68	69	70
71	72	73	74	75	76	77	78	79	80
81	82	83	84	85	86	87	88	89	90
91	92	93	94	95	96	97	98	99	100

Give the percent of the numbers 1 through 100 that satisfy each problem.

1. Mark numbers ≥ 81 with a red / _____%

2. Mark the evens with a blue / _____%

3. Mark the multiples of 5 with a green | _____%

4. Mark the factors of 72 with a yellow — _____%

5. Mark numbers < 11 with a black **X** _____%

Bonus: Numbers marked red, blue, and green. _____%

0-7682-2636-8 *Step-by-Step Fractions*

PARTing Shots

Solve by computing each percent.

Percent is a ratio based on 100 parts to a whole.

Example: 20 of the 25 students rode the bus

$\dfrac{20}{25} = \dfrac{80}{100}$ or 80% of the students rode the bus

1. On Tuesday, 6 of the 30 students were ill. What percent were ill? _____

2. The neighborhood carnival had 45 of the 50 families participate. What percent participated? _____

3. One serving of the dessert contained 22 grams of fat. A recommended daily value of fat is 66 grams. What percent of the daily value of fat was in the dessert serving? _____

4. The class collected $375. The goal was $500. What percent of the goal did the class collect? _____

5. Kayla had a $2.50-off coupon. The coupon equals what percent off the $10.00 price? _____

69

0-7682-2636-8 *Step-by-Step Fractions*

Math : English = Proportion : Analogy

A math proportion is similar to an English analogy.

Example: 1 : 24 = hour : day

Cross-products ➤ 1 day = 24 hours

Complete the following.

1. 1 : 7 = _____ : week

2. 1 : 36 = inch : _____

3. 1 : 12 = _____ : foot

4. 1 : 12 = _____ : year

5. 1 : 3 = foot : _____

6. 1 : _____ = dime : dollar

7. 1 : _____ = letter : alphabet

8. 1 : _____ = second : minute

9. 1 : _____ = year : decade

10. 1: _____ = degrees : circle

Bonus: Write two analogies that include number relationships.

11. 1 : _____ = _____ : _____

12. 1 : _____ = _____ : _____

70

0-7682-2636-8 *Step-by-Step Fractions*

Name ______________________________ Date ____________________

Tips

People often tip 15% or 20% in a restaurant. Change the percent to a fraction or a decimal.

Example: 15% of \$12.00 = $\frac{15}{100}$ x \$12 or \$1.80
= 0.15 x \$12 or \$1.80

1. Mikel planned to tip 15% on the \$32.00 bill. How much will he tip? ________

2. Alisha thought the tip should be 20%. How much would she tip? __________

Math Hint: Think of 15% as 10% + 5%. To find 10%, move the decimal left 1 place. To find 5%, halve the 10% amount: 10% of \$12.00 is \$1.20: 5% is 1/2 of \$1.20 or \$0.60, so the 15% tip would be \$1.80 (\$1.20 + \$0.60).

Use the shortcut to calculate 15% tips:

3. \$18.00 ________ + ________ = ___________
   10% 5%

4. \$24.40 ________ + ________ = ___________
   10% 5%

5. A shortcut for 20% is to move the decimal 1 place and then double the result. Use this shortcut to find a 20% tip on a \$36.00 bill. __________ → ____________
   10% double it

Fraction Scramble

The terms needed to complete the statements are scrambled in the Answer Bank.

1. $\frac{7}{5}$ is an _____ fraction.

2. 12 is the _____ common factor of 24 and 36.

3. $\frac{2}{3}$ has been reduced to _____ terms.

4. _____ is a ratio based on 100.

5. $\frac{35}{140} = \frac{}{4}$

6. $1\frac{2}{3} = \frac{}{3}$

7. $\frac{4}{5}$ and $\frac{5}{4}$ are _____.

8. 12 is the _____ common multiple of 3 and 4.

9. The product of 0.02 and 0.3 will have _____decimal places.

10. A _____is comparison of two quantities.

11. $3\frac{2}{3}$ is a _____number.

12. In the fraction $\frac{7}{9}$, 7 is the _____.

Answer Bank

tastereg   rpreomip   netcerp   slowet

eifv   eon   prolacescir   stale

there   orait   dimex   rateormun

   0-7682-2636-8 *Step-by-Step Fractions*